TEAM
FIRST
WINS

TEAM
FIRST
WINS

JULIE GOODENOUGH

Julie Goodenough

Gal 6:9

CENTER for BUILDING
Community

TEAM FIRST WINS

Copyright 2020 Gary D. McCaleb & Julie Goodenough

ISBN 978-0-578-64184-3

Printed in the United States of America

Cover design by Ron Hadfield and Todd Mullins.
Interior text design by Sandy Armstrong, Strong Design.

Abilene Christian University
ACU Box 29136
Abilene, TX 79699

To my super fans: My rock star husband, Rob,

and our incredible daughters,

Bailey (ACU '18, '19) and Macy (ACU '20).

Thank you for your support, sacrifices, love, and hugs.

You are my forever favorites!

2018–19 Women's Basketball Roster

No.	Name	CL.	Hometown/Previous School
#0	Kamryn Mraz	Fr.	Little River, TX/ Academy High School
#3	Dominique Golightly	Jr.	Chickasha, OK/Chickasha High School
#10	Breanna Wright	Jr.	Jarrell, TX/Jarrell High School
#11	Sara Williamson	SR	Rowlett, TX/Rockwall High School
#12	Josie Larson	So.	San Antonio, TX/Johnson High School
#13	Jazz Taylor	Jr.	Duncanville, TX/Collin Co JUCO
#14	Pamela Herrera	Jr.	El Paso, TX/Bel Air High School
#21	Kayla Galindo	So.	El Paso, TX/Riverside High School
#23	Jenna Cooper	Fr.	Claude, TX/Claude High School
#24	Diamond Willcot	Fr.	Cedar Hill, TX/South Grand Prairie High School
#25	Lexi Kirgan	Jr.	Bullard, TX/Bullard High School
#30	Anna McLeod	RS/Jr.	Houston, TX/La Tech
#31	Madi Miller	Fr.	Wylie, TX/Wylie High School
#32	Makayla Mabry	So.	San Antonio, TX/Incarnate Word High School
#33	Alyssa Adams	So.	San Antonio, TX/Johnson High School
#44	Lexie Ducat	RS/Jr.	Brock, TX/Rice University

Coaches

Julie Goodenough	University of Texas Arlington, Texas Tech University
Erika Lambert	College of Charleston, College of Charleston
Erik DeRoo	McPherson College, Fresno State
Drew Cole	Aurora University, Austin Peay University

Athletic Trainer

Maya Natori	Southeast Missouri State

Manager

Chris Garcia	

ABILENE CHRISTIAN WILDCATS

23-10 (13-5)

2018-19 BASKETBALL SCHEDULE

NOVEMBER

9	FRI	UNIV. OF THE SOUTHWEST	H	90-47 (W)
15	THUR	HOWARD PAYNE	H	98-43 (W)
17	SAT	EASTERN NM	H	78-46 (W)
20	TUES	NEW MEXICO ST.	A	58-46 (W)
23	FRI	TEXAS SOUTHERN	N	81-39 (W)
24	SAT	UTEP	A	70-69 (W)
28	WED	TULSA	A	63-75 (L)

DECEMBER

1	SAT	SCHREINER	H	90-43 (W)
8	SAT	ARKANSAS	H	68-80 (L)
17	MON	FLORIDA GULF COAST	A	65-81 (L)
29	SAT	TEXAS TECH	A	54-105 (L)

JANUARY

2	WED	NEW ORLEANS*	A	59-52 (W)
5	SAT	SAM HOUSTON*	A	91-79 (W)
9	WED	MCNEESE ST.*	H	109-52 (W)
12	SAT	SOUTHEASTERN LA*	A	71-74 (L)
16	WED	HOUSTON BAPTIST*	A	72-62 (W)
19	SAT	NORTHWESTERN ST*	A	72-63 (W)
23	WED	STEPHEN F. AUSTIN*	H	55-71 (L)
26	SAT	CENTRAL ARKANSAS*	H	77-70 (W)
30	WED	TEXAS A&M CC*	A	72-68 (W)

FEBRUARY

6	WED	LAMAR*	H	60-63 (L)
9	SAT	SAM HOUSTON*	H	63-72 (L)
13	WED	NICHOLLS ST*	HSU	76-66 (W)
16	SAT	INCARNATE WORD*	A	71-50 (W)
23	SAT	SOUTHEASTERN LA*	H	86-66 (W)
27	WED	TEXAS A&M CC*	H	72-55 (W)

MARCH

2	SAT	CENTRAL ARKANSAS*	A	67-65 (W)
6	WED	STEPHEN F. AUSTIN*	A	48-65 (L)
9	SAT	INCARNATE WORD*	H	102-53 (W)
15	FRI	CENTRAL ARKANSAS	N	82-54 (W)
16	SAT	LAMAR	N	88-79 (W)
17	SUN	TEXAS A&M CC	N	69-68 (W)
23	SAT	BAYLOR	A	38-95 (L)

FOREWORD

"If you want to go fast, go alone,
If you want to go far, you need a team."
—John Wooden

The importance of "a team" seems to be so easily over-looked. As a result, we instead focus on individual effort, personal accomplishments, and self-made champions.

Coach Wooden's statement could be supported by the fact that his UCLA basketball team did "go far," winning 10 national championships in a span of 12 years (1964–1975). Some might argue that those wins were due to some great individual athletes, but another Wooden quote would respond, "A player who makes a team great is more valuable than a great player."

The word "team" is frequently used as a metaphor far beyond the sports world. Businesses refer to their "sales team," hospitals have referred to their collective work in providing health care as a "team effort" of doctors, nurses and support staff. Groups as large as a city and as small as one family use the team metaphor to describe the value of working together.

And that is where Coach Julie Goodenough's personal journal can provide valuable insight. Too often the team is reduced to only what is seen: the uniforms, the game performances, the statistics. This book provides a look into what is not seen, with an account of not only the "game days" but the weeks, even months, when there were no games, and also the days, and hours, before the games and after the games, in the locker room and on the bus. And it is a story that provides a year-long verification of Coach Wooden's statement: "If you want to go far, you need a team."

On one occasion, I had the opportunity to spend some time with the team with none of the coaches or any others present, and with no reference to Coach Goodenough's personal journal, or this book, asked each player to write her own spontaneous responses to a few questions, without discussion or interaction with the other players. The questions were along the theme of "What do you think the fans who come to your games see?" and "What do you think the fans never see?" Each player handed her paper to me, and their responses were not shared with other players, or any coaches. I did make them aware at the outset that I was interested in their individual thoughts which might be used in a project on which I was currently working.

As I have looked over the players' comments, several themes have emerged that seem to fit into the "unseen" essentials for not only this team, but any "team," whether athletic, corporate, religious or family. With each theme, I have included elaboration, using only written comments from the members of the ACU Women's Basketball team.

Time

- "They can't see the hours spent shooting free throws and 3s and layups. They can't see the hours spent during breaks spending time together growing our chemistry."
- "We spend a lot of time not only working on the court but building a foundation to truly understand one another."
- "I've had a lot of great memories on the court, but my favorite memories are off the court with my teammates, time away from basketball and spending time with one another is crucial."

Open Communication

- "We try to understand one another and openly communicate. We aren't just there for basketball."
- "The way we communicate with each other is inspiring."
- "Our team talks about God. We do a great job of communicating this."
- "We communicate well."

Love and Respect

- "Most importantly, how much we love and respect one another."
- "All of us respect each other on and off the court. We all know that no matter what, we are all there for each other. It's a huge thing to have coaches respect us the way we respect them."
- "We show the difference it makes when a team loves each other."
- "We love the game and we love and respect one another."

Babe Ruth, a great athlete, long celebrated for his individual success, was quoted as saying, "The way a team plays as a whole determines its success."

My first impression was that Ruth's statement seemed extremely obvious; however, on reflection, I have decided that there is a deeper truth hidden within.

To restate the sentence in a way that reveals its wisdom, I would write:

"Team is far more difficult to attain than
is winning."

I believe it is possible for a group of players to achieve some level of success without ever truly achieving "team," which allows them to realize a higher and broader level of success.

To illustrate, consider the following paraphrase of a familiar quotation by inserting "team" instead of the usual word:

Within true "teams" you will find patience and kindness, and you will find no conceit or pride. In a true "team" you will find no rudeness or selfishness. True "teams" keep no record of wrongs. True "teams" never give up. (Based on 1 Corinthians 13:4–7.)

It's easier to merely work on the things that are noted in game charts and statistics, and they are important. But that group of players will never know what might have been. And I would argue that the players who commit to achieve the level of a true team will find that the measurable (and unmeasurable) outcomes far surpass what they would otherwise have been.

Amitai Etzioni has observed "Communities do not come in digital switches, on or off: they come in varying degrees of thickness."

Based on the responses from this team, Time, Open Communication, and Love and Respect emerged very prominently, making a strong case for their essentiality as unseen immeasurables, or we might say components of "thickness" for a team.

But two other words deserve honorable mention: Caring and Chemistry.

Caring

- "We are a family and truly care about each other."
- "We have each other's back no matter what life throws at us."
- "We are very protective of each other."

Chemistry
(which has been called another word for "trust")

- "Our chemistry comes from the amount of time we spend with each other."

Finally, there was one other theme that the members of this team, this exceptional small community, knew was absolutely essential: Leadership. Two comments speak eloquently for the team:

- "The most important factor that has contributed to ACU's Women's Basketball history is a great, strong leader and we have that in Coach Goodenough."
- "ACU Women's Basketball success can be credited to our coach. She has laid a foundation and culture for this team that is so much more than basketball. Her mentorship to us as women gives us success. When you come to ACU you have the choice to buy into the culture or leave. If you stay, I've learned you can win championships AND become a better person. Essentially, all of the credit begins with Coach Goodenough's leadership."

When Coach Goodenough first gave me the opportunity to read her personal journal, I was struck with three thoughts:

1. How rare it is to have such a day-by-day candid account of a championship season from the handwritten journal of the coach rather than a third-party professional writer.

2. How rare it is for the coach (or anyone) to maintain the discipline to keep such a journal amid constant distractions over such a long span of time (and to capture details, both ups and downs) so well.

3. How rare it is to have an opportunity for the Center for Building Community to publish such a document that is both an interesting and readable story for families and fans who treasure the memories of this singular season and provide for others a personal, yet metaphorical insight into building community—whether in sports, business, family, city or nation.

And if you don't feel you have time to read the entire book, at least read the **Team Meeting Notes**, December 16.

Executive Director
Center for Building Community

ACKNOWLEDGEMENTS

The 2017–18 season followed back-to-back Southland
Conference Championship teams. We defined it as
our "reloading" season, as we sought to find our iden-
tity in what seemed to take the entire year. Spring 2017
graduation left us without the talents and personalities
of our Division I era building blocks, forwards, Suzzy
and Lizzy Dimba, shooter, Alexis Mason, and center,
Sydney Shelstead. To say we were a little short handed
was an understatement. However, through successes
and failures, that team learned to fight through battles
together and win games that no one expected them to
win. They led our program to the first ever Southland

Conference Tournament and won a first-round game! They exceeded expectations.

At the end of each basketball season, you have an opportunity to reflect on the total body of work and then to begin dreaming and imagining about what the next season will hold for your program. We finished the season on a roll. I had such a feeling of optimism preparing for summer workouts and the addition of our next class, which was highlighted by Lexie Ducat, who had completed her redshirt season. The future was bright for sure!

One regular day in April, Dr. Gary McCaleb and I, as we so often do, were discussing the potential of our team. We shared a common feeling that this 18–19 squad could be really special! We agreed that with the right chemistry and a team-first mentality, this team had the talent to make history for the ACU women's basketball program. Dr. McCaleb suggested that I keep notes and document this season, just in case our intuition was correct and it actually turned out to be a season to remember. Thank you so much, Dr. McCaleb, for your friendship, encouragement, and for the wisdom to keep a journal! I would not have done that on my own, nor would I have even thought about turning the journal into a book!

Thank you, Lea Watkins, for adding this project to your long list of responsibilities. I appreciate your typing, editing, printing, and suggestions for this book, as well as your keen attention to detail.

Thank you to my parents, Conrad and Betty, for introducing me to sports and great work ethic. My love for basketball began at a very young age as I shot hoops at our house with my parents as rebounders. Because of your selfless "no job is not my job" example, you have been my inspiration to strive to be the best version of myself. I also appreciate seeing you in Moody cheering on the Wildcats!

I have been blessed with the rare opportunity to be a head coach at the college level for 25 years. My support system at home, Rob, Bailey, and Macy, has allowed me to do what I love. Thank you for all the hours you have been in the gym cheering me on! I love the quality time that we enjoy together and I appreciate you for sharing me with so many others. Thank you also for opening our home and our family to so many players throughout the years. I love you very much and could not do this job without your support, nor would I even want to!

My assistant coaches deserve a huge "thank you." Erika Lambert, Erik DeRoo, and Drew Cole, you are relentless workers and ambitious teachers who help to facilitate my vision for this program. Let's continue standing up for our culture and holding our team accountable both on and off the court.

Thank you to our incredible mentors for loving our players and being daily examples of Christian role models! And a special shout out to our amazing male scout team! I am 100% certain we would not have been prepared for the huge battles this season without you challenging us in practice. (The names of those in each of these two groups may be found in the Appendix.)

This amazing season would not have happened without the commitment and dedication of the teams and players who came before. A special thanks to Renata Marquez, Whitney West Swinford, Paris Webb, Suzzy Dimba, Lizzy Dimba, Alexis Mason, Sydney Shelstead, Sierra Allen, Cailyn Byrd and Taudencia Oluoch. Thank you for trusting me and for investing in this program and in this university. Always remember "see ball-see girl," "low hips-high hands," "**control the controllables**," and **TEAM FIRST WINS!** You are the embodiment of "Those who stay will be Champions."

Thank you to my athletic director, Allen Ward, and our president, Dr. Phil Schubert, for being forward-thinking visionaries for ACU athletics and for your Godly leadership on this campus. Your support is invaluable to me!

The ACU athletic administrators, staff and coaches are a relentless support system for our program. Thank you for the fantastic family atmosphere in which I am blessed to work every day. Your cheers, texts, and hugs do not go unnoticed and are so appreciated.

Wildcat Nation, thank you for turning out in big numbers in Katy and then again in Waco! Our players loved playing in front of such great crowds! You have established a new precedent for basketball support at ACU!

Thank you to the members of the 2019 Southland Conference Tournament Championship team. What a blessing to be a part of this season with each of you! Thank you for believing in me, our philosophy, your teammates, yourself, and in the hope that God had immeasurable blessings for us if we would be faithful and strive for excellence to honor Him. My prayer for you is that your faithfulness this year through victories, heartbreak, pain, laughter, adversity, and teamwork, will only be the beginning of a life filled with blessings through your commitment to Jesus.

I am thankful for the grace of God and for the precious gift of coaching and the privilege to use it as my ministry.

THE JOURNAL

The following pages contain the unedited,
handwritten notes of Coach Julie Goodenough

June 3 (a.m.)

Welcomed our team back to campus including 6 new players and 10 returners

New:

- *Jazz Taylor: 5'6 salty point guard from Collin Co (Rice)*
- *Anna McLeod: 5'11 pure shooter from Houston (La Tech—will sit out this year)*
- *Jenna Cooper: 6'0 post; set Texas High School State Tournament record with 22 rebounds in 1 game; from Claude, TX; has ONLY been coached by her dad!*
- *Kam Mraz: 5'5 scoring point guard with great court vision; from Little River Academy*
- *Madi Miller: 5'9 shooting guard who got lost in a very talented 2018 DFW recruiting class from Wylie High School, Wylie, TX (good addition for us)*
- *Diamond Willcot: 5'11 post from Cedar Hill High School; huge personality, good athlete; will be a role player*

I have a parent-only meeting on move-in day to reassure them that we will love their daughters and help them become their best on the court, in the classroom, in their relationships, and in their walk with Jesus. I am always transparent with the fact that they can now stop texting and emailing us on their child's behalf. Communication should be directly from their daughters (that often causes big eyes). The final message is for them to understand that we are beginning with the end in mind and have our sights set on the NCAA Tournament which requires a SLC Tournament Championship. They all smile and nod, but I bring that to a screeching halt when I tell them that all parents (including me!) would rather their child be all conference than the team win conference. They can't admit it publically, but it is so true. That's just how we parents are; I want them to understand that this is a business that will function as one unit, one team, and NOT 16 individuals. If they can remember that and remind their daughters of this throughout this season, it will be very helpful.

TEAM FIRST WINS
is our mantra and our philosophy

June 3 (p.m.)

*The next meeting of the summer is with the new players. I want them to know without a doubt that we live daily to be **Godly Women Striving for Excellence** (Mission Statement). The biggest Core Value for them to embrace* over our six-week summer schedule is **Control the Controllables.** *They need to focus on only those things that they can control.*

The main 3:

1. *Energy (Effort)*
2. *Attitude (You choose your attitude everyday)*
3. *Communication (Talking to teammates/coaches)*

1st Team Meeting: (So excited to start this season with this team!)

In the first meeting, players voiced a real passion for setting our top team goal as an NCAA Tournament appearance. To make the NCAA Tournament, we will have to win the Southland Conference Tournament. A difficult task, but one which our team wants to strive for.

I emphasized our Core Values and Standards of Excellence (see Appendix).

Integrity, Grit, Control the Controllables: *the ones our team suggests we need to focus on improving the most!*

I decided to create an application process for the Team Captain selection this year. We cannot enter this season without designated leaders. All players were given the opportunity to apply. Eight players applied, interviewed

with the coaching staff, and basically campaigned for
their seat for 6 weeks through workouts (basketball and
strength training, assisting with our summer youth and
team camps, and community service).

June 28

Summer workouts are always skill-development
intensive. As we work with new players, a few weaknesses
are exposed:

- Lack of communication
- Stances are not athletic
- Not accustomed to playing at a fast pace which is
  forced on you by the shot clock
- Tentative about full speed for Fear of Messing Up
  (FoMU)

However, we have 6 new players who can really score—
which is my _favorite skill!!_

Summer camps were the best-run camps since I've been at
ACU, maybe because we have more players than ever (16)
or maybe because they are being led by good juniors and
a senior, or we have an elevated level of character with
this team. Didn't make excuses—invested in campers.

July 2

Captain Reveal

At the end of our 6 weeks, the players joined the staff on the football field to watch the captain video reveal on the big screen. (Wildcat Stadium has changed so much of what we are able to do with our team—1ˢᵗ Class, wonderful.) We were even joined by Dr. McCaleb, who took pictures of our new captains.

Our players loved the reveal! Cheered for our captains! Seth and Erik created an awesome video that announced the 4 captains:

Brea! Dom! Lexie! And Jazz!

July 5

As we prepare to leave town as a staff to recruit, I am not concerned at all about leaving the team in the hands of our captains. They are so passionate about their new roles and about winning. They will be difference-makers for this season!

July Assistant Coaches Staff Meeting

My notes for staff meeting:

Trust is huge in this business

- *Work every job like it's the best job of your life— love every piece of it.*
- *This is a "people" business. You deal with people ALL THE TIME—recruiting, players, media, etc.*
- *Everyone cares about how you treat them. Some may care about the weather, playing time, social media, etc., but everyone will ALWAYS care about being treated right.*
- *Being loyal is being a good assistant coach—make your head coach's job easier; assistants assist the head coach.*
- *Support staff supports the staff.*
- *Your staff needs to be a "family" if you expect your program to be.*
- *You need good players, but you need good people too.*
- *Use your connections, even if it's a person to get to a person—hold on to those connections.*
- *The "right move" is bigger than what's on the sur-face—it doesn't matter what the perception of others is if it's right for you.*
- *Be in the moment . . . it's your moment.*
- *We are all products of our experiences.*

- *Life and coaching aren't perfect—timing is vital; you are where you are because it's where you are supposed to be right now—it's preparing you for your next eventual opportunity.*
- *Love the jobs everyone else hates to do—sweep the floor, hand write envelopes, pick up donuts for workouts.*
- *Trust God, follow God.*
- *Are you really working as hard as you can? Be where your feet are!*
- *Have balance; you can't cheat your family.*
- *You are a father, husband, coach, etc.—it's a hard balance at times but it's not impossible at all.*
- *If you preach "family" in the locker room, you better do it at home too—our loved ones are the easiest people to neglect because we always know they're going to be there. That's not fair. (I still struggle with balancing family and team responsibilities.)*

July 12

Recruiting is so much fun—evaluating future Wildcats and navigating the recruiting process. I love to travel around the country in ACU recruiting apparel and have strangers approach me in airports who have a story about when they attended ACU or when their kids were in school at ACU. ACU is so Big-Time around the country! Here are a couple of my favorite stories from this summer:

- *Waiting in the Louisville airport, a gentleman approached me and asked if I was an ACU alum. I explained that I'm the women's basketball coach. He said his younger brother was a wild trouble-maker from Sweetwater and probably would have ended up in jail if he had turned down the offer to play football at ACU for Wally Bullington!*

- *Another man spoke to me in the Dulles airport when he saw my ACU backpack. He explained that he ran into Dr. Schubert at an event in Dallas and introduced his son to Phil. Told his son that he was classmates at ACU with Phil. Fast forward 2 years, this dad was sitting in Cullen with his son when Dr. Schubert spoke to the group as part of New Student Orientation. The son asked his dad if that was the guy he had met a couple of years ago! His dad said yes and the son said "You didn't tell me he was the ACU president! You are friends with the president of my school!"*

2018 Caravan

July 31

Joe T. Garcia's & Hard Eight BBQ

Love talking about our team to our donors and fans in the DFW area. They are the fans who geographically are actually able to make it to events on our campus. The majority of the folks in attendance had also attended home football games in Wildcat Stadium—such a game changer for all of us in athletics but also generates even more fellowship and pride for ACU alums! Macy was able to go with me and serve as my personal texter while I drove. And she is a great make-up and hair advisor, too.

August 3 & 4

I love camps and look forward to them all, but team camp is awesome for sure! We had 40 high school teams participate this year! The most so far! We have reserved space in all 4 Money Recreation Center gyms and Moody. At least 400 players here on campus, using facilities, and being around our staff and players. But the best part is just the opportunity to showcase our campus and wonderful facilities to the 2,500+ fans (friends and family) who come to the games in support of their teams. Always an awesome way to end the summer! Levelland beat

Frienship in the final (Frienship was defending champ from last summer!).

August 15

We have a new A.D. on campus. Allen Ward from Murray State! He has convinced me already through the interview process and phone calls that he is a basketball guy and understands how success for Men's Basketball (MBB) and Women's Basketball (WBB) can really make an impact financially and in support of an athletics program. One of his first tasks he says is to upgrade Moody! So awesome!

August 21

Freshman move-in! I love it!

Jenna Cooper/Kamryn Mraz: Room 229 Gardner

Madi Miller/Diamond Willcot: Room 168 Gardner

Cooper Family: including mom, dad, grandparents and Jonathan

Kam: Tiffany, John Berry, little brothers Kaden and Casey, Maci and Kam's mom (moms are busy decorating—JC and Kam want the workout schedule for the 1st week— love it!)

Madi: Mom, dad (Laura and Darrin); mom is not happy about move-in process but probably just nervous about drop off

Diamond: Jacqueline and Mike and two brothers. Mom doing some moving of furniture and figuring out décor

Diamond and Madi are both stressed out about conditioning tests. (Pretty normal!)

Freshman perspectives: They have no clue what this year will bring. No way they can know without living it. Then they will become sophomores! This is a really good class.

August 23

Taylor Morgan: 2020 All-Saints Point Guard

Unofficial visit on campus with her dad. This may be the first piece to an amazing recruiting class and we will need to hit a home-run because of who we have to replace in our 2020 graduation class (Brea, Dom, Jazz, Lexie and Pam).

Boom—Taylor committed!! Get them on campus and we have a good chance to convince them to commit! This is a really good get! She will be the cornerstone for this 2020 class!

August 24

Returners Move In—1st Meeting! Friday of Wildcat Week

5–6 p.m.

Basically, each team meeting has some type of boundary breaker—a question that each player answers while her teammates all listen respectfully. I like to hear everyone's voice and love to listen to them share their opinions, and often times their hearts, in our boundary breaker segments.

1ˢᵗ Team Meeting has to establish the tone, expectations and vision for the season. Each player receives their team notebook and we cover different sections over the first 2 weeks of school. I don't want them to "wonder" what our program stands for, or believes in, or who we play for, so we give detailed information to them in their notebooks. We spend extensive time on our core values throughout the season and those values are normally the first item of business covered in the notebooks. Other pieces of information included are academic policies and expectations, standards of excellence, social media policy, team travel standards, and practice expectations.

Each player has a jar of marbles above their locker. The marbles represent each week remaining in their ACU basketball career. The 1st meeting the seniors have 28 marbles, thus 28 weeks 'til the final regular season game (JRS=80, SO=132, FR=184). This gives the players (and staff) a visual everyday of how quickly time goes by and it's also a reminder to enjoy the process!

7–8 p.m.

ACU Fest—Erik, Drew and I set up a table in Rec Center to recruit male scout team guys. We had 30 freshman guys sign up who are interested in helping us. Awesome! If we end up with a squad of 10–12 that would be great. We have 5 returners to begin with. Our male scout team is issued workout gear and a pair of basketball shoes. They are instrumental to our success because of their speed and size. Without them I'm convinced that our team would struggle to reach our potential! These guys are good basketball players and also high-character men who just want to be a part of something special. And they get a good workout with our practices as well. Because they help our team so much, they also receive championship rings when our team wins a championship!

8:30 p.m.

Rylee Young is a 5th grader who has been a loyal camper and ball-girl for the past 3 years. Tonight, her dad, Ron, let me ride on the back of his motorcycle into Moody to fire up our freshman class of 2022 and get them to come out and cheer for the Wildcats this season! It was a blast (more than 1000 new students)! I love the loud energy in Moody!

August 29

1st Team Workout

Players concerned about conditioning tests but oh so fun to have all 16 players in a basketball practice! This is going to be so fun! Early basketball workouts will always include ballhandling, passing, and layup drills. These skills are the foundation for everything else that we do on the offensive side of the ball. We do absolutely emphasize defense and work on it daily, however, scoring is how you win ballgames, so preseason skill workouts are offensive intensive.

September 1

1st Football Game at Baylor

Oh my, what fun and a chance to see what an impact students and fans can make on a sporting event. The Baylor Line for Baylor football is such an impressive student section—great energy. Each freshman knows the dances and cheers for every song and chant (these are learned in freshman orientation). I'm sure our ACU game day folks are taking great notes on this atmosphere!

September 3

September means preseason for basketball teams, but also Sept. evaluations and contacts. My staff and I will be on the road extensively in Texas and Oklahoma watching athletic period basketball practices. Not all states have athletic periods during their normal school day, which is just another way Texas sets itself apart. Texas athletics are the best because of the emphasis from the high schools, the quality of coaches, and the governance of the UIL! We watch practices, visit w/coaches and after the school day ends, are able to do home visits with the recruits and their families. My assistant coaches cover so many practices during Sept. I will attend 13 high school practices and one jr. college workout, which will be fewer than all 3 of my assistants! They are such hard workers!

September 6

Team Meeting
<u>*11:00 a.m.*</u>

Team Meeting Topic—Lyrics from "Who You Are" by Unspoken

> "You can never fall too hard
> So fast, so far
> That you can't get back
> When you're lost
> Where you are is never too late
> So bad, so much
> That you can't change who you are."

a. *Forgive self—ask for forgiveness—God/others are involved in the process of forgiveness.*
b. *Face the consequence of mistakes.*
c. *Have some people around you who can help you through tough times. We hope and pray that each player has at least one coach and one teammate that they trust and believe will have their back if they need anything. My staff and I are intentionally*

available for our players at work and also after hours. We feel a strong obligation to coach them, but also to be Christian mentors as well!

September 7

<u>7:25 a.m.</u>

*Our team participates in **High 5 Friday** at Taylor Elementary School 2-3x a year. This was a cold, rainy morning where the students did not want to get out of their cars. Our players dressed in rain gear, rain boots and, equipped with umbrellas, helped dozens of children get out of their cars and walk into the school.*

September 8

I will not miss any preseason basketball workouts for September evaluations but will miss a couple of swimming workouts.

Sept- Monday........ 6 a.m. Track Workout/Full Team Workout
Tuesday........ Basketball Individual Workouts
Wednesday.... Basketball Full Team Workout
Thursday...... Swimming
Friday.......... Pickup

3 days a week the players are in the weight room with our strength coach, Bret Miguez.

September 11

Allen High School

Tyler Jackson 2020 Guard
Zoe McCray 2020 Post
Good young players as well

September 13

Edmond North

Graycen Holden 2020 Post, plays for the Swarm. Such a strong post who can also handle the ball. High character, loves Jesus.

Christian Heritage Academy

Rylee Langerman 2020 Guard. Also Swarm. Great family. Twin brother, Ryan, could be on our scout team. Tough as nails! Has alopecia—doesn't affect her at all on the court.

September 15

Mudslinger—Annual Team Run in Mud

*We work each year at this event, then our team and staff
run the course together. Muddiest event ever—rained
all week so no extra water needed! Several groups who
volunteered to work didn't show up because of the harsh
conditions. So glad that we were there to help with our
group of 20!*

*We ran the 5K in deep mud pits, getting so muddy from
head to toe. Lexie, Jazz, Kam and Madi made a race
of it and tried hard to beat each other. I stayed with
the team to make sure everyone worked hard. Another
interesting challenge of getting them out of their comfort
zones. Makayla, Alyssa, and Lexi did not seem to enjoy
the day. Even with encouragement, they had a hard time
not being grumpy about cold and mud. Interesting in
those situations when players focus on themselves and
forget that we are all doing the same and all getting wet
and muddy. Brea, Madi, Anna, Dom, and DeRoo worked
hard after the run to unstick cars.*

September 18

Amarillo High School

Zayla Tinner 2020 Utility Player, can play 2, 3 or 4!

September 24

Argyle High School

Rhyle McKinney 2020 Guard, Super talented point guard who scores at all levels

September 24

Disability Resources, Inc. (DRI) Chapel

I love our time with DRI. Some of the players are initially pretty uncomfortable there because they haven't spent time around grownups with disabilities. Pam always seems right at home giving hugs and listening. Makayla, Josie and Kam also have a sweet spirit about helping and laughing with the folks. We leave blessed for sure. Ian, Phillip and Patrick were the most talkative, like normal, along with our fav Beth! Her sister Joy led singing! They told us that they are excited to perform the National Anthem at some of our games again this season. This group is called BELL PEPPERS.

September 29

Big Prospect Day

Hosted 13 recruits and their families. Campus Tour, Wildcat Country, Photoshoot, Wildcat Football Walk, Tailgate, BBQ. Great fellowship in the lawn by our office.

Football game. Team introduced after 1st quarter. Wonderful crowd! Great conversations with recruits and their families!

Sat in the suite with the Rick Wessel family after halftime. Love having fans/alums speak so kindly about athletics and our team. By the way, our football suites are so beautiful and give a fantastic vantage point for watching the football games! The Wessel family has done so much to advance athletics with gifts like the incredible scoreboard at Wildcat Stadium.

Freshman Follies/Family Weekend

One of my non-negotiables is that our freshmen perform in ACU FRESHMAN FOLLIES. They always stress out about it, but thank me later. HaHa.

Diamond helped to choreograph dance moves for her group in "Umbrella." They were so cute with yellow rain coats and umbrellas. She and Madi were stars! Jenna and

*Kam were in a group who sang hits from "Mamma Mia."
Neither act won and they were mad about it! Mission
accomplished—forced to work out of their comfort zones
and ended up being very committed and competitive
for their teams. I love seeing the players realize they can
actually do more than they think they can. The team all
attended dress rehearsal in support. Also in attendance
for dress rehearsal were the McCalebs.*

September 30

1st Official Basketball Practice

30 days of workouts before 1st game

No more track or pool (for a while)

*Makayla has had a great preseason. Alyssa has been really
positive and had a good attitude in preseason. Josie is still
fighting demons of thinking she can only make 3s and
not layups.*

*Madi is proving to be a tough player physically, but needs
to be more coachable. She is hard on herself, but uses
that as an excuse of why she doesn't respond to coaching
verbally. But she will be good as a freshman!*

Jenna can really shoot 3s. I need to find ways to play her.

Of course, Brea and Dom are really in good shape, healthy knees, shots are on, good toughness. Sara has been the best surprise! Love her attitude and great work ethic!! In April I gave her the ultimatum of changing her negative attitude and influence or she would not get to be in our program this year. She has been so positive and usually 1st to respond verbally in practice and even 1st to respond to texts and emails. She has come a long way. It's a long season, but she has begun in a positive and professional manner (22 weeks left in her ACU career).

October 3

All-Sports Student-Athlete Chapel—1st Wednesday of Each Month

Erik worked hard the month of September to get video from every ACU team practice. I worked on collecting video from "Dynamic Duos" on campus—mainly from the athletic department.

Opened chapel with highlights. I entered chapel on a Bird—love those new scooters that are so popular on ACU campus!

Spoke about how being too focused on success, we may not see adversity creeping into our blind spots (see notes from speech following). Need people to step into those areas and warn us or have tough conversations to help us. "Dynamic Duos" video was to represent people in our dept. (& McCalebs) who have each other's back, have each other's interests at heart.

October 3, 2018

ACU STUDENT-ATHLETE CHAPEL NOTES—"Blind Spots"

—Start off by recognizing some groups:

Freshmen—raise your right hand!! Welcome—we are so glad that you chose to be a part of something really special. **Give them 1 clap**

—Guarantee this will be the hardest year of your life so far!

—Not a better place in the world though than ACU to go through that transition! You have a lot of people HERE who genuinely care about you and who are praying for you.

Sophomores—raise your left hand!! **Give them 2 claps**

—You are survivors right? Made it to the sophomore season!

—*You have a big responsibility now to mentor and encourage these freshmen.*

—*You may think you are all that, but you are not that far removed from being a freshman—use your experience to cheer them on and make sure they know **they got this!***

Juniors??—throw your Wildcat sign!!!! **Let's Go 3 claps!**

—*Do you know what you really are? You are **JUNIOR** Srs!!*

—*You are not a Sr, but rather learning how to be a Sr.*

—*This season you should be about learning from them but also making sure it is the greatest year of their career! **HONOR THEM!!** They deserve that from you and you will appreciate the favor returned to you by the underclassmen when you are a SR!*

Seniors—please stand! **Let's give it up for our srs.**

—*It is quite an accomplishment to make it to your SR year and we are proud of you and everyone in this room wants this final year as a Wildcat to be your most memorable.*

—*Give your best effort to leave a legacy for future players & have NO REGRETS!!!!!*

—*Know that this year will fly by! SR Sara stand up. **Sara has 22 weeks** left in her career which will go by so fast!*

Football Srs you have 6.5 weeks!!!!! *Make the most of it!!!!!*

—***Time is our most valuable currency—spend it wisely!!!!!***

—*Think about all of us in this room. We are part of a Christian DI athletic department.*

—*For us to succeed at this level we have to be driven, ambitious and competitive. As achievers, we must strive for excellence in the classrooms as well as on the fields.*

—*We take care of ourselves, monitor sleep, lift hard in weight room, are serious about nutrition, striving for excellence—to be the best version of ourselves.*

—***We should want to be a part of something special! Win conference! Win conference tourney! NCAA Tournament!! Be All Conference, 4.0 in the classroom. Set personal records: Ring by Spring!!***

Awesome stuff. *We get extremely disciplined and focused and stay in our lane and even put up blinders to keep distractions away and this is all good, isn't it? We can't accomplish much if:*

—*We don't go all in!*

—*We must maximize the present. Stay focused on moving forward.*

—But often times with this kind of tunnel vision, what happens is we get so focused and result & goal oriented that we forget to check our **blind spots!**

Just like driving a car—yes we are mostly focused on what is in front of us through the windshield and we also check the rearview mirror and side view mirror, but we get so busy moving forward at a fast pace that we forget about what can be in the **blind spot**, that's when accidents happen.

We get so caught up in where we are trying to go, that we don't look over our shoulder.

3 things that can cause a derailment, or an accident if we don't check in our <u>personal</u> **blind spots:**

Arrogance   **Selfishness**   **Bitterness**

1. **Arrogance** can be: thinking we are Big Time, full of our self, don't need others to hold us accountable. Better than others, resisting coaching, **stubborn, don't think we need to change**
   - The Bible tells us that arrogance can lead to failures.
   - Proverbs 16:18—First pride, then the crash, the bigger the ego the harder the fall!

- *God has a unique path just for us but when we think our plan is better—we make bad choices and miss those blessings that he has in store for us.*
- **Be obedient**. *Listen to God's plan=allow people who care about you to help you and coach you.*
- <u>Rom. 12:3</u>—**As God's messenger I give each of you God's Warning; Be honest in your estimate of yourselves, measuring <u>your value by how much faith God has given you.</u>**

2. **Selfishness**—*As humans, it seems natural to want more, to want what others have. But when we compare ourselves to others and to what they have, we **lose** focus on what we can control which is **us!***
   - **Our attitude, and our energy are the 2 things we have total control over.**
   - *We can't control others, so our focus is on being the best version of ourselves, better today than we were yesterday.*
   - *The Bible warns about selfishness in Philippians 2:3. **Don't be selfish, don't live to make a good impression on others. Be humble, thinking of others as better than yourself.***
   - **CS Lewis says, "Humility is not thinking less of yourself, just thinking of yourself less."**

3. <u>Bitterness</u> *can result in being mad about everything. We blame others. Why is she starting over me??*

   - *Something really bad might actually happen to you—injury, accident, illness—but you still can't let bitterness eat away inside.*
   - *If you don't handle it appropriately, it will prevent you from those special accomplishments and put you on a destructive path.*
   - *If you are holding something over another person, staying mad at them, chances are they don't even realize it and it's not bothering them at all. It is a very unhealthy mindset for you that can cause setbacks in your life, when bitterness is in your **blind spot.***
   - *To remove bitterness=choose <u>Forgiveness</u> to unlock the handcuffs of bitterness. Release its stronghold. <u>Ephesians 4:31–32</u> provides a good reminder: **Instead be kind to each other, tenderhearted, forgiving one another, just as God has forgiven you because you belong to Christ.** Pray to forgive wrongdoers, and let God handle those situations so you can get back on the path moving forward.*

*What I believe helps us stay in God's will and be aware of objects in our **blind spots** are Christian friends, buddies,* *teammates, family who care enough to stand in that gap and make us aware of danger in our **blind spots.** These are people who love and care about us and want us to **pursue excellence to be the best version of ourselves**.*

Depending on the size of your team it's hard to hold everyone accountable. So, on our team, you need to have one buddy in whom you invest daily—on and off the court. You cheer, encourage, and also have tough discussions with your buddy to help them stay on the right path—a path filled with blessings. On our team this season, everyone has been assigned a "buddy." You can tell who their buddies are because they are twinning with their buddy today!

Do you have a friend like that? Do you monitor a friend's blind spot?

*I'm not talking about **virtual friends** on social media. A real friend is someone who can **actually give you a high 5 or a hug**.*

*We have a lot to accomplish—it **absolutely** takes our **very BEST effort**—and with help from others and being willing to help others, <u>We</u> can Glorify God as we pursue the Greatest year ever for ACU ATHLETICS!*

So today, I leave you with a challenge to choose **obedience, humility and forgiveness** and stand in the **blind spot** for a teammate, a friend.

Let's see what **awesomeness** is really ahead for us as individuals and teams and as the ACU Athletic Department.

Go Wildcats!

October 4

Team Meeting

Topic—from Jon Gordon's book—"The Power of the Positive Team"
Ch. 5 "Positive teams remove and transform negativity"

What was emphasized from this chapter is how it goes along with our core value of **Control the Controllables**. *Before the season even begins we have to collectively choose to NOT allow negativity in our locker room.*

Right now everything is good, we are undefeated, no one is unhappy about playing time and no one is behind in classes because we haven't started travelling yet.

How will we handle adversity? Because we will encounter adversity!

We have to choose to confront it, remove it or transform it. Ignoring adversity will not be an option. We would like to have such a strong culture that negativity will not feel welcome and either leave on its own or be transformed into something positive.

We implemented the "No complaining rule," which is also inspired by Jon Gordon. We will not complain unless we have a plan for a solution. This changes the mindset to focus on the solution—where we want to be, and not on the problem.

Our team did a great job discussing how negativity and negative words can sabotage our team and our ability to succeed.

We decided as a team to begin monitoring our own and each other's words. We have choices over what words to use and we want to speak words that are positive and uplifting at all times. We also discussed choosing to view our responsibilities with a heart of gratitude. We will choose to be thankful and not whiny. Two other changes in our language will be using the phrase "Get to" instead of "Have to" and replacing "Problems" with "Challenges."

*Really thinking about being positive is also a mentality of putting the **Team First**. For each person in our program, our words and actions are a reflection of our culture.*

October 7

Wildcat Mentor Reception, 2–3 p.m., Wildcat Stadium

Each player tells me what their "dream job" is. I match them with a female Christian mentor in Abilene who has that job. At our reception they meet and visit with their mentors (see Appendix) over cookies and lemonade. This is only our 2nd year to have this program, but it has been very positively received by players and mentors. I want our players to have another female role model in town who will also be a Christian example. We invite mentors to our end-of-season banquet and they are also recognized at one of our home games. The mentors were given a vest like the team and we took pictures with their mentors.

October 9 –10

Southland Conference Media Days

Great trip talking to Joe Golding en route, and good to see other conference coaches.

Found out we are 6th in preseason poll. Great motivation to Exceed Expectations! If our sights are on 1st and a bid to NCAA tourney, low expectations by our opponents is a good reminder of how far we have to grow on the court and in unity to reach our lofty goals!

October 10

Etiquette Dinner

*Jennifer Ellison taught us about appropriate table manners, interview attire, phone manners, how important "thank you" and "thank you notes" are, even in 2018! The food was delicious! The five-course dinner was prepared by our resident chef at ACU. Love seeing our players dressed up and again working on improving skills that will help them in their adulthood. Our team is very noticeable when we travel together. As we visit restaurants and stay in hotels, we want to be aware that we are always leaving an impression and could be the only ACU interaction that these people ever have. It takes a little extra effort to look professional, be polite, and use proper manners. But if we are putting our **Team First**, we can't always just make the easiest decision when given choices. We have to be aware of making the choices and engaging in behaviors that are best for our team. **Team First Wins** doesn't just apply to on-court actions but is a mentality that we have all day, every day.*

October 11

Team Meeting

Practices of Unshakeable Women—Guard your Hearts!!

A. Hearts—Proverbs 4:23

The Heart is our soul and our emotions

The Heart is where God speaks to you

Access to your heart is through your eyes and your ears. If we are not careful about what we allow in, God's instruction could be compromised. We could be distracted from God's word and plan.

The information and images that you let in will determine your heart's language: gossip, negative words, cultural norms, filthy words, inappropriate music & tv, movies. In other words, "garbage in/out."

Let the word of God, the Bible, be the guideline to what you let into your heart!

Fill your hearts with love, joy, peace, confidence, truth, so there literally won't be room for the other.

B. Engage your minds—Philippians 4:8

This is Cailyn Byrd's favorite verse!!!! Noble, right, pure, lovely, admirable, excellent, praiseworthy.

Boredom can lead us to Facebook, Twitter, Netflix, etc. We just start looking to be amused or just to pass time. Be self-disciplined to focus on Godly things.

Find 3 things a week to look forward to!

Guarding your hearts and minds also goes along with the Iceberg Principle (see Appendix). We have to protect and foster our values and beliefs which are "under the surface."

October 12

Hall of Fame Dinner

Sara was my guest for the ACU Athletics Hall of Fame dinner. She looked so pretty and carried herself with confidence in a packed room of fans and alumni. We were seated with Stan Lambert, Allen and Sharon Ward, Deonna Shake and President Schubert.

It was a 1ˢᵗ Class event and the recipients were so genuine and sweet in their memories of being Wildcat athletes. The love and joy they exude made me so proud to coach at ACU! This is truly a special Christ-centered place! Sara seemed to enjoy the evening and thanked me for taking her. I heard her the next day at the parade and our team tailgate telling her teammates about what she had listened to at the banquet. I challenged her to strive for excellence every day this season to lead us to another championship, which would make her the 1st and only ACU Wildcat to win 3 Division I Championships. I believe she is motivated to do just that!

October 13

Prospect Day

Hosting 13 recruits and families. A messy, rainy day started with the Homecoming parade. Our team handled it well (not near as bad after running a 5K in the mud—perspective!!). We hosted recruits to a photo shoot, campus tour under umbrellas, and tailgate in Gym C. A fun, fun day—then off to the football game.

These prospect days are a big production. Coach Lambert coordinates our recruiting visits. Coach DeRoo coordinates photo shoots and creates mailouts and graphics from the photos. Coach Cole helps with tours and all set up and break down. I am responsible for providing the food! I love our assistant coaches and appreciate their work ethic and creativity! My job is made awesome by the opportunity to work alongside this staff.

Recruiting future players is a huge undertaking that continues the entire year. You never take a break from recruiting. It is the lifeblood of our program! I am thrilled with our amazing Wildcat Stadium! The ability to invite recruits to on-campus visits now on a football game day has transformed our recruiting efforts! The energy, the tailgating, and the tremendous fan support on a home football game day is an incredible example to recruits of the support and excitement for ACU athletics!

October 16

Annual Pumpkin Unload

Each year we unload roughly 50,000 lbs. of pumpkins from the back of a trailer for the Disability Resources, Inc. fund raiser—the Pumpkin Patch. As rainy and messy as the parade had been, this day was even rainier! I like jumping in the trailer with my gloves on, to set the pace and speed of the unload. Very similar to the Mudslinger, several groups who signed up to volunteer were no shows because of the rainy weather. I told my team that we would once again practice integrity and fulfill our commitment. The job was made more difficult than normal because of the cold rain and muddy lawn, but we got it all unloaded in 1 ½ hours. There was no way the DRI folks could help in these bad conditions. Made us thankful to be healthy and strong!

As individuals, this was a tough job, but having the mentality that this was about our team serving our DRI friends made the challenging weather fun!

October 18

Each team captain was asked to lead one team chapel this fall. Lexie Ducat was first to lead one. She spoke on "being yourself." "Don't try to be someone you are not," Lexie said. She shared about how at Rice she tried hard to fit in and please others. She expressed how she feels that at ACU she can be true to herself and be someone her teammates and coaches can count on. She wants to be a servant teammate and also a leader of integrity for our team. Her message was heart felt and well received!

October 19 – 20

ACU Fall Break.

*19th: 7:25 a.m. Before workout—once again started day in the rain. An ACU group signed up for **High 5 Friday** at Taylor Elementary, not realizing that it was Fall Break.*

We took their place, lined up on the sidewalk outside of Taylor and cheered and high-fived students coming to school. We wore rain boots and held umbrellas as we watched students sprint from their cars to give and get high 5s from our team. Sweet, sweet time! There to bless, but left blessed!

20th: Began our day driving to Camp Butman in Merkel. We divided into 2 groups—completed elements of a low ropes course.

Foot tag, thumb wars, animal toss-together. I placed Sara, Brea, Alyssa with my group. I believe that my relationship with them, in particular, is very important for our team this year. I wanted them to see me get to be a follower and problem solver alongside them. Today was another activity for working outside of our comfort zones!

Kam was a good vocal leader for our group. Madi and Alyssa approached tasks with "I don't think I can do this" but each time were able to do it and do the job well! Jazz and Lexie worked very well together. Hope they will get closer to their teammates this season.

We were challenged with balancing on a wire, swinging on a rope and landing inside hula hoops, lifting a tire over a telephone pole and lowering it without touching the pole.

Teams came together to hold a long, thick rope in a circle—they held the rope with both hands waist high. I walked on the rope around the circle using their heads to balance. Somehow they were able to hold the rope so strongly that I didn't fall. Cool element! If players on the opposite side of the circle from where I was walking would have relaxed it would put more pressure on the 2 or 3 who were bearing my weight. Each member of the team had to do their job well.

All activities were such that all teammates had to work together to achieve success.

*Just like basketball, putting the **Team First Wins!***

October 21

This fall workout schedule has been a challenge—fitting workouts and lifting around our class schedules. Our players are learning how to prioritize their time, meals, and equally important as well, their sleep.

October Calendar

Mondays—	*6–8 a.m. Workout*
	2–3 Afternoon Ind.
Tuesdays—	*5:45 a.m. Weights*
	6–9 p.m. Team Workout
Wednesdays—	*5–7 p.m. Team Workout*

Thursdays—	*5:45 a.m. Team Workout*
	11 a.m. Team Chapel
	8 a.m./3 p.m. 2 Weight lifting Groups

October 22

Week before UTA scrimmage

Workouts are at high tempo, high reps. Freshmen are pretty lost with all of the plays we are running. Getting ready for scrimmage with UTA. Hope to hit shots and move forward with communication and defensive intensity.

October 25

Chapel with all ACU Women's Teams

Oct—(Pink) Breast Cancer Awareness month. Hendrick reps asked us to write letters to patients who are going through cancer treatments. Gave Sara a good chance to talk about how strong her mom had been thru her treatments. Sara's mom is clearly her rock.

ACU Women's Team Chapel is always a fun way to see all of the other female athletes and get caught up on how their teams are doing.

October 26

Shared with captains to choose to be Thermostats rather than Thermometers. They are to set the culture that will influence their teammates. One of my favorite Habitudes from Tim Elmore is the Thermostat vs. Thermometer. Each player on our team is either a thermostat or a thermometer. The leaders have to assume the role of a thermostat, which is a person who controls the climate in a room, in a practice, in all team activities. They set a tone that fosters and cultivates the core values of our program. Followers are merely thermometers that reflect the climate around them. As leaders of our team, always and in all ways, our captains have to put our **Team First** *regarding how they respond. Their actions will need to be rooted in our team core values. They will not be able to react like a thermometer, who would simply mirror the temperature in the room.*

October 27

UTA Scrimmage

"Deer in the Headlights" was apparent for the freshmen. We had too many turnovers and UTA shot 45%. Revealed deficiencies on defense for sure: poor stances, not talking,

closeouts not close enough to shooters, face cuts, used hands too much to defend drives.

Good feedback to help restructure practice plans to get ready for scrimmage against our scout team on Nov. 2.

October 29

6 a.m. Workout

2–3 p.m. Video sessions instead of individuals. We met with our guards at 2 p.m. and with our post players at 3 p.m. Before film, I asked team to rate communication on team, 1 being you just know everyone's name, 10 being excellent, with no room for improvement with communication and relationships on the team.

2 p.m. Guards average of 6.0, voiced concerns about not knowing who they could really trust. Also some were afraid to speak up sometimes, in certain situations for fear of a teammate disagreeing with them.

3 p.m. Posts average 5.5, some of same thoughts as the guards, but also mentioned selfishness caused people not to spend enough time on getting to know each other. I think we have done a lot to build team chemistry, but this is a reminder that Culture and Connectiveness need to be worked on daily. We obviously have some work to do with better communication and growing the love, respect and chemistry of our team.

November 1

*Brea led chapel. Spoke on being consistent. Easier to trust someone who is consistent in attitude and work ethic. She wants her teammates to view her as a player who is "all in" every day and also a player who is unwavering in her commitment to the team. A player who strives to be consistent has a great chance to bring the best version of herself everyday instead of every once in a while. Brea is the most consistent worker on our team, so this was such a great topic for her! She values teamwork and really does put our **Team First**, which I believe is the intrinsic motivator for her desire to be consistent.*

November 3

Practice Under New Lights in Moody

Allen did it! He had new lights installed in Moody. It looks so awesome! Has to be worth 4–6 pts. per game!! Allen's experience being the athletic director at Murray State has given him a great perspective on what is necessary for basketball programs to be successful.

Week of 1st Game—We have to get minds ready for it

November 9

Univ. Of Southwest

Theme this week—*Positive teams remove and transform negativity (from Jon Gordon, "The Power of a Positive Team")

Everything is good right now while we are undefeated. Playing time isn't an issue yet.

How well will we handle adversity when it strikes? Because it will be hard to anticipate all the ways it will affect us. So as a team we must always be ready to take the following two-step process to deal with adversity:

Step One: Confront
Step Two: Remove or Transform

We cannot allow Energy Vampires, those players, coaches who zap the energy away because of negativity.

Cannot allow empty complaints, complaining focuses on the problem.

We need to focus on solutions.

Continue using <u>GET TO</u> instead of <u>HAVE TO</u>. Use the terminology "challenges" instead of "problems."

Win #1 (vs. Non-D1 so win expected)

Really liked how Brea was our coach and vocal leader. She needed to establish herself as the floor general from Game 1 and she did so in a convincing manner. Makayla! She had a great preseason—so glad she played well today, just like she has been practicing. Exciting 1st game! (11 made 3s by our team.)

November 12

Team divided into 4 groups to visit elementary schools that will be attending our inaugural Wildcat Kid Day on Nov. 15. Game will tipoff at 11 a.m.

5 schools have committed to bus several grades in for the game.

Each school has been given 3-4 of our players to make signs for and to especially cheer for. Pizza & H2O will be served for lunch.

Thursday, November 15

Win #2

What a great win—good teamwork, fight, energy. Lexie showed great signs of being a scoring threat—led in scoring and rebs!! (14 pts—13 rebs) Hit twelve 3s as a team.

Game was well played and exciting. However, the excitement of the game actually failed in comparison to the AMAZING crowd! We will for sure make Wildcat Kid Day an annual event! The children were incredible! Their cheers, dancing, and energy were just fantastic. The official box read 3500 attendance. My assistant coaches threw candy to the crowd 45 mins before the game and the kids went crazy! Their excitement not only continued but also escalated until the final buzzer!

Our players were a bit shell shocked at the volume level to start the game, but eventually relaxed and played a great game. An example of how an energetic crowd can really inspire and motivate the team!

November 17

Win #3

Guards played great—shot ready—really good job getting ball into the paint. Lexie D. had another good rebounding effort. Alyssa was ready to compete today. She ran the floor so well and was a huge presence in the paint. It was so good to play solid at home again before we travel for the 1st time (all next week). (9 made 3s)

November 21

Dinner at Pam's house

Kayla's mom also helped with dinner. Great time with their families and just being with our team. Our players are doing better with thanks and showing appreciation.

November 22

What a great Thanksgiving dinner @ El Paso Country Club. Angela (Mooney) knew a UTEP donor who helped us make a reservation at the El Paso CC for lunch. We had our families, Jim and Charlene Shewmaker and Robin with us. Total party was 46 people. Our bus driver Robin—he's the best. He said "this is the best meal I have ever had."

We have requested Robin Walls as our bus driver for the last four seasons and we will continue to do so! He has told me several times that even after he retires he will still drive our team! Robin has a nickname for each player who is currently on our team and every player we have had over the past four seasons! He is really unlike any driver I have had! He does his research before each trip while studying our team itinerary. We stay on time as he uses the best and safest routes to each destination. Once he delivers us to the arena for our games, he parks the bus then comes back to cheer for our team! He loves to coach the players up during the games and is a very genuine source of encouragement at all times when we are with him. He is also a faithful fan at our home games.

Win #5 v. Texas Southern

We jumped out to a great 16–4 first quarter and never looked back! We expected their pressure to slow us down but it actually sped us up and allowed lots of paint balls and layups. Very good team win! Dominated the rebounds, which also led to high percentage shots. Makayla had 10 rebs—she is going to be so good!!

Win #6 v. UTEP

<u>Oh</u> my goodness—what a fun win! <u>Again</u> jumped out to a great lead in first quarter 23–8. We didn't know how to handle it though—lost 2nd and 3rd quarters. Came back and battled so hard in 4th quarter—4 players in double digits. Brea continues playing at a high level with verbal commands and court vision. 14 made 3s.

We had to get the ball back in the final minute. UTEP inbounds the ball to a post player near half court. She didn't want to dribble, and actually stepped across the line into the backcourt—Wildcats' ball! This set up what would be our game winner! Sometimes you can make plays and play well through adversity, but you still may need a little luck to go your way!

November 28

I was so proud at how our team handled a week on the road when we traveled to Las Cruses and El Paso, but the trip to Tulsa was not good. We suffered 1st loss but not just on the scoreboard. Looked so disinterested before game and during. I believed before the game that we could beat this Tulsa team, but not without fight and focus. We lacked intangibles (grit and effort) and teamwork too. For the 1st time this season I am a little concerned about lack of "coaches" on the floor. Brea cannot be the only vocal leader during the games. We have 4 captains and really need all 4 to get out of their comfort zones to coach and encourage during games. Have to get mojo back to play toughest game of the year—hosting Arkansas on Sat., Dec. 1.

November 29

Team Chapel

Navy Seals go thru an incredibly difficult training. They are the ultimate special forces unit, in my opinion, so obviously their training would be so extreme that only the very best survive. During training if they don't want to go through the rigorous training any longer—they can ring a bell and go home. Don't want to get up early, swim in freezing ocean water, be yelled at, be in pain any longer—**"Ring the Bell!"**

My message to our team is to make Arkansas **"Ring the Bell."** Be aggressive, dictate, annoy them and force players to **Ring the Bell!** It will have to be a combined team effort—a relentless mindset to protect our home court and through grit and putting the **Team First**, we will force them one player at a time to **"Ring the Bell."**

December 1

Second Loss/First Loss at Home, vs. Arkansas

My pregame fire-up reiterated the power of team and let's make Arkansas **"Ring the Bell."** Great crowd! The fans and students really showed up—Christmas Slam. Even had SNOW outside! Everything was set up for us to take advantage of home court advantage.

We led at the end of the 1st quarter. Down at half-time. Makayla was in foul trouble which allowed Arkansas to defend only 3 shooters on perimeter. Great team effort to win 3rd quarter! 4th quarter debacle—Bad Coaching. I let our players get fatigued, caused some careless turnovers and bad shots, we couldn't defend their speed in transition after our turnovers.

I have to help our 7th, 8th, 9th players improve in practice. I didn't have confidence to play them in this close game. I have to teach and train them (Madi, Josie, Kirgan, Alyssa) better in practice. That is my responsibility and this game revealed my deficiencies.

We hosted an SEC opponent for the 1st time ever! Because we kept it so close this may be the last time to host an SEC opponent! Other schools in their league may not want to come to Abilene, TX. This atmosphere was tremendous and allowed our team to stay positive and continue fighting the entire game. If we can get SEC players out of their comfort zone, we can dictate on defense on a regular basis!

December 16

Flying to play Florida Gulf Coast, this will be the best team on our schedule, (first flight of the season)

Kam's 2nd flight ever! Always love to be able to give players new experiences!

Freshman Diamond left her wallet in her car. Alicia, who was driving a van, took her back to ACU to find it. The rest of us are checking into airport and going thru security.

Good practice at a private H.S. gym. We had a good time at the beach. So many people taking advantage of the sun! The players enjoyed laying out and finding an ice cream vendor.

Bailey and Macy were my beach buddies! I love my girls and am so thankful when their schedules allow them to be with me on road trips. They are my inspiration to be the best coach that I can possibly be! This job requires me to sacrifice a lot of time away from my husband and our girls. So I decided early in my career that for their sacrifices of not always having me around, I would honor them by striving for excellence as a coach! If we are going to be apart, it needs to be for a very good reason. They are my biggest supporters, always!

Team meeting topic—It all starts with love

The only way we will win and be successful on a consistent basis is to love each other and to love what we are doing! We will face obstacles this entire season. We have to love each other enough to fight and persevere through the adversities. If we want to be GREAT, love is required. We need to seek ways to serve each other and through that *service they will know we care. Great teammates make their teammates feel important and they show them how much they matter. This is a good time to remind ourselves to put TEAM & TEAMMATES first—**TEAM FIRST WINS**.*

December 17

My goodness was love and service demonstrated! Great bench energy! Another loss, but what a great game! Our team proved that they can play with a really good team! Great atmosphere—good program and game day to try to mimic! At shoot-around, Sara was so silly! We play music for warmup and during shooting drills at shoot around. At the end, we were cranking out music loudly over their sound system—Bailey as the DJ. When "All I Want for Christmas" by Mariah Carey came on, Sara started an animated lip sync version with dancing. It was great—our team loved it! I was laughing so hard! I wondered how we would respond in the game after something like that, after being so silly at shoot-around?! Well, Sara was a beast—scored 22 pts, 9 of 10 FGs, 4–4 FTs.

Learned quickly that she and her team can play well and play focused even when they are loose and silly.

Our demise was giving up 15 offensive rebounds. Still a lot to be proud of in this battle with literally only 5 ACU fans present, and an arena packed with FGCU fans.

We are now going into the longest Christmas break we have had. I am concerned about losing chemistry, conditioning, strength, and focus. We have 8 days off. Upon returning, we will have to get ready for Tech. How we return from this break, both mentally and physically, will impact the length of future Christmas breaks.

December 29

Defining Moment—Game at Texas Tech

Most embarrassing game I have coached in a decade. Unbelievable!

Couldn't hit a shot. Struggled to defend the paint. No player played with energy or confidence. No encouragement from bench players. Nothing seemed to work for us, while everything Tech did worked. This is a Tech team who has not experienced much success this season.

Players wouldn't respond to coaching. No talking. Playing a Big 12 team is nothing new for our program, but may be too much for this team.

I was pretty hot, livid actually, after the game. When asked about lackluster effort and lack of teamwork, the players responded that they were scared and intimidated. Initially, I want to scream about that lame excuse, but I can tell in a lot of their eyes that they really were scared. WHY?!? They practiced well. They learned the scout—good game plan!

Good lesson about this team—even though we have captains, no one led this team from the locker room into this daunting battle. If they don't really believe BEFORE the battle, they will lose hope easily when things don't go well in the game.

My staff and I have to fill them with confidence as we prepare for battles. We must eliminate excuses so that the players are completely confident and without any doubts before the game begins.

2019

January 1

University of New Orleans—Sam Houston State

Preseason 6th (Our players were very displeased about being ranked 6th in Southland Preseason Poll. Must be in Top 4 = to get a bye in the conference tournament).

Conference is about to begin!

With help from generous donors we are flying to New Orleans. Our bus driver, Robin, is meeting us at NOLA airport. Play UNO then drive to Huntsville for Sam Houston game.

Three critical questions about this trip: 1) Will we be able to recover from Tech failure? 2) Can we move forward as a team? 3) Can our staff preparation fill the team with confidence?

In our team meeting:

Believe in self.
Believe in teammates.
Believe in game plan.

Courage in sports means giving 100% for your team—No Excuses! Control what you can control—for God's glory. Give best version of self! Courage—focus on what you have control over. Prepare and be ready to give your best effort.

Staff and players shared "One Word" for 2019 (see Appendix). Great sharing of self. Love hearing from their hearts. Choosing one word to help you stay focused on your goals is a Jon Gordon activity.

January 2

UNO Game

We only scored 2 pts in entire 2nd quarter, but oh my, what an incredible 1st Conference Win! You have to win at home and steal some road wins if you want to have a special season! This is one we may have stolen! 3 posts fouled out! Played short-handed most of game with 32 fouls called! Showed toughness and extreme resistance to quit! Loved the Grit! **"GRIT DON'T QUIT"** *was said more than a few times during the second half! 59–52 ACU over UNO*

Drive to Sam Houston—of course Robin found beignets along the way in Baton Rouge!! Robin is the best driver!

January 5

2–0 on the road nonetheless! Twelve made 3s! all by Dom, Brea and Makayla. Ducat, Alyssa and Makayla all fouled out. In this game our players weren't rattled at all when plagued by foul trouble. We knew from UNO experience that we would be fine! Weather the storm, stay the course and follow the game plan.

Fearless guard play! Brea, Sara (7–10 fg), Dom (5–11 fg) may be BEST guard TRIO in the SLC! Too early to make that bold prediction, but I truly believe it!

91–79 ACU defeats Sam Houston St.

January 6

We attended my church, Pioneer Drive Baptist, as a team. Challenged to expect struggles in 2019 but know blessings are promised if we follow the right path, seek to serve others.

Great dinner and fellowship at Denise Barnett's. Such great fans. Mentor for Anna and Alyssa.

January 8

Fun evening at Rosa's with McCalebs and friends. Our players each spoke on their "One Words." Dr. McCaleb does a tremendous job bridging the gap between our players and special fans. They are so sweet and hospitable to our team each year during the Christmas holiday.

January 9

Home Game v. McNeese

We must win our first Home SLC game because you have to win the first one to win them all. Winning at home is key to having a special season.

Win #3 comes in an impressive offensive showing! 14 made 3s (by 8 different players!). 27 assists—awesome display of teamwork and confidence.

109 points scored. Most pts scored v. DI opponent, most pts scored in an SLC game so far! Ducat speaking up a lot in timeouts!

I had anticipated a great game v. McNeese. Felt good the whole week leading up to the game. 2–0.

109–52 ACU over McNeese

January 12

SLC Loss at Southeastern Louisiana

We have now lost in Hammond 2 years in a row, basically déjà vu!!! We jumped out to a healthy lead, then struggled to play together as a team in the 2nd half! Needed to score on last possession (just like last season!!). I felt good about the chance for Sara to redeem herself from poor performance at SLU last year. I called sideline out of bounds for her to drive for layup or kickback to Brea. She drove and got her shot blocked instead of kickback to Brea, who was wide open for 3-pt. shot. It's easy to watch from the sideline and you think you would know what to do and would actually make the right read in that situation.

It wasn't the correct read based on how the defense responded, but I do like that Sara wanted to be big in that moment. This loss will be one that could hurt us down the stretch and prevent us from a Championship or even a bye in the SLC Tourney, but time will tell if we will use this setback to unite our team or will we allow a spirit of doubt to creep in? We will find out quickly when we play again on the road in Houston next week.

71–74 loss at SLU

January 15

Classes begin this week for the spring semester. We will leave on Tuesday and return late at night on Saturday. This journey will take us into battles at Houston Baptist and Northwestern State. Travel is not always as glamorous as it may seem. Traveling as a team is really fun and is where many of the best memories are made, but it is difficult as well.

Our long Tuesday through Saturday trip over Thanksgiving week gave us a glimpse of what this week will be like, and we went 3–0 then! The difference, though, in these two trips is that this week is the first week of the semester. Since our players are so serious about doing well academically, the timing of this trip has created some stress. Riding on the bus and sleeping in hotels all week can also cause stiffness and a lack of sleep. This will be a great test to focus on what we can control and that is mental toughness and learning our scouting reports.

January 15

Team Meeting in Locker Room

Prov. 4:23

The heart is our soul and our emotions. The heart is where God speaks to you. Protect the access to your heart, your soul and your mind—be careful about what goes in there or God can be compromised. The Bible is the guideline to what we should let in—stay away from bad language, gossip, filthy songs, music, movies, TV. "Garbage In, Garbage Out" are the words of my own grandmother. I believe she understood about keeping your mind and heart clear for Jesus.

Phil 4:8: "Finally brothers and sisters, whatever is true, whatever is noble, whatever is right, whatever is pure, whatever is lovely, whatever is admirable, if anything is excellent or praiseworthy, think about such things.

Engage your minds in only what is noble, right, pure, lovely, admirable, excellent, praiseworthy. Boredom can lead us to Facebook, Twitter, Shapchat, etc., for amusement. Guard your hearts and minds! Protect what is under the surface. (ICEBERG Principle, See Appendix)

January 20

What a successful trip! So proud of how our team handled huge road swing. Tough places to play—Houston Baptist/ NSU. The response to SLU loss was great team chemistry— seem to have each other's interests at heart. Selling **TEAM FIRST WINS** *daily. That will be the key along with GRIT that can keep us heading in the right direction. Lots of encouragement and laughter on this trip. I love hearing the positive sounds coming from the back of the bus!*

@ HBU—72–63
@ NSU—72–62

SFA and then UCA both at home this week.

Huge week (I say that a lot). When you have high expectations, you have to be demanding and push yourself and players and staff to be uncomfortable pretty much daily.

January 23

As we prepare for what we know will be a huge battle, I feel confident about the players' focus on the task at hand. Stephen F. Austin is a well-coached team with talented individual players.

One of my favorite movies is "The Patriot" with Mel Gibson. He tells two of his young sons to "Aim Small, Miss Small." He was referring to shooting a target with a rifle, but we used that phrase to set our sights on paying attention to details. Don't get caught up in the hype of the game, but rather aim small, focus on the details of our game plan. If we don't hit the target, we will still get close (miss small!).

January 24

Team Chapel—11 a.m.

Rough day following a bad loss to SFA last night. We were ready, but seemed to play not to lose rather than playing with the fire and urgency to win. And to add to the disappointment in our own performance, we are today hearing about allegations in the athletics department. These include racial tension, academic fraud, and sexual misconduct. We do not know any full stories, but are reminded that everything— every decision, our behaviors, our actions—are all a reflection on ACU, on this program, and on each other. **TEAM FIRST WINS** *continues to drive us to make choices with integrity and to seek to serve Christ in all of our decisions. In the same way, our team is a part of and a reflection of the athletics department and we will support the other teams through their adversities, while striving to be the best version of ourselves. We can't condone bad decisions but rather we can live in such a way that others see Jesus through us. We can absolutely get attention for our team and our department by winning games, but also for doing what is right and being women of integrity.*

January 26

UCA, Good Alumni Event

Diaper Dash at halftime—BEST PROMO! Following the game, we had our annual alumni event coordinated by Erika with the help of Erik and Drew. It's great to catch up with our former players but also meet players who were here before any of us were. This program has enjoyed success on the court throughout its history, but my favorite part about meeting former players is learning about how being an ACU Wildcat changed the trajectory of their lives. ACU transforms hearts and lives.

THEME for UCA Game: "There is no time for Ease and Comfort. It is time to Dare and Endure." Winston Churchill.

We know UCA will always bring a great defensive effort. Lost 3 times to them last season. Have to protect home court. Jumped to a big halftime lead, then the Kamry Orr show began. The Churchill quote came to life in the 4th quarter! Had to stay uncomfortable and show Endurance until the final buzzer!

77–70 ACU over UCA

January 27

*Woke up thinking about how Sara played v. UCA. She is surprising me with her leadership and toughness. We say **GRIT DON'T QUIT** and that is how she led us last night. She played with confidence you would expect from a Sr. and a Sr. who is realizing that her time as an ACU Wildcat is really only a few weeks longer. Good for her leading us to a hard-fought battle over UCA in front of alums and her former teammates.*

January 30

Goodness, Texas A&M Corpus Christi is a scary team. They could win every game left on their schedule!! We had a great scoring 1ˢᵗ half in their gym. Took a 14 pt. lead to locker room at halftime. And good thing! Makayla and Sara both were in foul trouble which forced Alyssa and Madi into action! Alyssa was aggressive to draw fouls down the stretch when our shots weren't falling. Madi has guts! May not play as smart as we want her to yet but she has guts for sure! Made a huge 3 and a huge assist to Dom when we had to have it. Our depth won the game tonight! We will need depth to reach our goal of finishing in the Top 3 in the conference.

February 6

Lamar

*Lamar could be called our Achilles heel. When our schedule only allows us to play them once a year, they usually get the better of us. Loved the fight tonight. No quit. **Team First** mentality tonight, but, dadgum, just make a play in the 4ᵗʰ to play to win. We are at home and Makayla cannot score because she won't shoot. Madi is out of sorts, maybe psyched herself out about playing* *preseason favorite for the 1ˢᵗ time. (This is a girl who never made the high school playoffs but wants to win so badly!)*

We just couldn't overcome the defensive pressure in the 4ᵗʰ, which they converted into high percentage baskets too many times.

The Sr./veteran leadership of Lamar is what we need to emulate next season but learning together how to win these games this year will be key to future growth and success. If we see Lamar in SLC Tourney, we need the confidence that we can beat them by simply getting defensive stops so they cannot get into their press. I also think we can score in transition after our defensive stops. Their full court pressure after they scored can be so fatiguing both mentally and physically.

Lost 60–63

February 9

Turning Point/Or Demise, Defining Moment For Sure

So humiliated at home by Sam Houston. Lost 63–72 (1 of the best crowds of the year because in men's game was #1 Sam Houston vs #2 ACU!).

Our team lost in quarters 2, 3 and 4. Crazy game where team looked disinterested, dysfunctional, no confidence, and ill prepared. I was nauseated during game by inability to reach and motivate Makayla, Sara or Dom. Three of the best players in the league and certainly in the gym, are looking at me with no confidence or no interest, one or the other. We just dropped a key game in this championship hunt—AT HOME!

Following the game, I calmly expressed my concerns and regrets on the game and said we are not leaving until we figure out as a team why we weren't ready to play, weren't interested in playing and why we just played with no passion.

It seemed like a dam broke and words began to fly, literally back and forth across the locker room! Accusations, tears, fears, hurt feelings, lack of respect—you name it—it was voiced! I literally sat on my stool and listened to shots being fired for 45 min. to an hour. How about "Aim Small, Miss Small?!" There were very candid and detailed discussions that hit the bullseye!

Basically, the meeting ended with everyone crying, or at least teary eyed.

And I said, "This is our defining moment. This either breaks us or carries us to a conference championship."

We either get mad and be immature about what was just spoken or we grow up, recommit to respecting each other again and go make HISTORY!

There is no in between! I really believe mediocrity is out of the question.

We TANK after this or we WIN BIG! I don't think there will be an in between.

We will trust in His plan, but know in our hearts we have to, or get to, choose to follow His lead, His path. We won't move forward on our own. Time to give up some of our control, my control, to Jesus. God has a plan to grow this team, through Big Success or perhaps Big Failure. Either way—Let's Go!

February 13

HSU

v. Nicholls

Sing Song Week so our game moved to HSU to play defending SLC Tourney Champs—Nicholls.

90 minutes before every game we meet in the locker room for meditation/visualization.

HSU allowed us to use the Cowgirls' locker room. This is the same locker room that my players were in for 9 years when I coached the HSU Cowgirls.

Following this prep time together, the team goes to the locker room door to head downstairs for pregame warmup. At this point they have 80 minutes 'til tipoff so the game clock was at 80:00. However, the door knob is malfunctioning?? It will not open! I call downstairs to the HSU athletic office to ask them to send someone upstairs to open the door. It turns out that it won't work on the outside of door either!! Funny really—Madi, Kam and Josie were making jokes about crawling thru ceiling tiles to get out. Josie wants to lift Pam up to crawl through the ceiling to get help. Gathered in locker room with the entire team—lots of jokes about rationing granola bars and spending the night (not much talk about the game at all!).

We listen to several solutions being suggested by HSU personnel on the other side of the door, but have no input or control from our side. 45 minutes later they cut a hole in the door to remove the doorknob. Our normal pregame warmup was cut in half and we were only allowed to add 5 minutes to the pregame warmup time, so we had around 38:00 to warm up!

This was a great exercise in controlling what we could control. Our players chose to have fun with the lock instead of freaking out or getting angry.

Well, it was all for the best! We were forced to hang out together in the locker room for 45 mins! Exactly what we needed—spend time together making light of a situation out of our control.

Earlier that day, Sara had been told in front of the team in shoot-around that she would NOT start. Madi would start instead. Sara was emotionally upset about the decision and it was seen by her physical reaction to the news. This change in the lineup was based on behavior and performance the past week.

I was concerned about how she would respond! In the game, in 25 minutes of playing time, Sara scored 24 pts! She may have been inspired to prove me wrong, but whatever the case was, she was really good and helped us beat Nicholls on a Neutral Court!

Our team had 9 made 3s and fought off a Nicholls team with reigning SLC Player of the Year Cassidy Barrios, and a team who shot 35 FTs (to our 15!!!)!

What a special game (@ HSU locked in the locker room). Big-time win but great example of a refocused team who played so in sync!

*Began **GLUE GIRL** award after this game. We will give bottle of glue to a player who daily exemplifies GLUE (adhesive) and does what is necessary to hold team together!*

*We talked about what it means to be a **GLUE GIRL** in team meeting on February 12.*

Webster's dictionary defines glue as "an adhesive." The physics definition of adhesive is "a force that exists in the area of contact between unlike bodies and that acts to unite them."

Or we could define it simply as "glue holds stuff together."

Who is the glue on our team? Who holds our team together? Who keeps us focused? Who does little things in practices and games to make our team successful?

*These are the questions I asked our team in the meeting. Well, the answer would be our **GLUE GIRLS**.*

*How do we recognize a **GLUE GIRL?** They would be seen doing these types of things:*

- *Taking charges*
- *Diving for loose balls*

- *Hitting crucial FTs (because they put in extra shooting)*
- *Blocking out on every shot*
- *Constantly talking to teammates*
- *Cheering from the bench*
- *Giving High 5s*
- *Setting great screens*

A **GLUE GIRL** *doesn't care about her own stats or playing time. All they care about is the team's success and know they did everything they could to contribute to that success. Every team needs* **GLUE GIRLS!** *Every team needs players who will consistently sacrifice for their team.* **GLUE GIRLS** *are even more important when a team is facing adversity. To make a serious run at winning a championship, we need to appreciate and recognize our valuable* **GLUE GIRLS**—*every day!*

Makayla Mabry is our first **GLUE GIRL**—*she hit 4 crucial 3-pt. shots, had 4 rebounds and 0 turnovers!*

February 16

Dominated University of Incarnate Word in San Antonio

Pregame UIW Speech:

Our focus before the game was to play like **GEESE**. *Geese are great teammates. As soon as a flock takes flight to head south for the winter, they instinctively form a "V" formation. This pattern allows the flock to fly further than they could alone because of the additional lift and reduction of air resistance. This is a great example of how our team has a better chance to win when we work together.*

With a flock, the lead goose changes as they get fatigued. Another goose will fly to the tip of the V to take over. Our team needs different leaders to step up during the game as other leaders maybe get in foul trouble or just need to catch their breath.

Geese also honk at each other, which is what you hear as they fly overhead. I believe they are communicating and encouraging one another. Everyone on our team can be cheerleaders for their teammates. Encouragement can help us through tough minutes in a game. And the encouragement also shows how much you care about your teammates and our team.

Alyssa was AWESOME in front of her hometown crowd. Loved the confidence she exhibited. Won 71–50.

[I drove home immediately after the game to catch the end of Sing Song. The past 2 years that GATA won

Sing Song, ACU WBB won Championships! Is there a correlation? GATA 3rd place.

Maybe we don't win regular season championship since GATA doesn't win, but we can win SLC Tourney Champ w/out help from anyone!]

February 20

Some of the thoughts racing through my mind:

Home Stretch—fatigued but still fighting

Core Value check

We have potential to jockey for 3 or 4 seed

Accountable—players speaking out in practice, calling on better effort, better execution from teammates.

***Controlling what we can control**, going to tutorials, not waiting 'til last minute to ask for academic help*

Integrity—being honest, trustworthy, players seem respectful and trusting of each other

Loyal—believing in game prep, teammates and coaches

In preparation for SLU and TAMCC—this is still the team with a potential to win the conference

February 23

+20 on Southeastern Louisiana University, 86–66

Twelve made 3s to dominate SLU. Revenge was OBVIOUSLY a big factor. Played not just with passion but a focus like we haven't seen this season. Exciting to see a KILLER instinct developing in this team.

February 27

72–55

Top 2 players of TAMCC didn't make trip to Abilene. Don't know why they were suspended but reminds me of how awesome my players are. Yes, they make mistakes, but I really believe they are becoming responsible teammates and believe in themselves, their teammates and our system.

We beat Corpus handily and with poise and confidence. 6 players combined for 10 made 3s. Also won the rebound contest 35–26.

In our pregame talk, we discussed how important loving and serving each other would be in this game and for the rest of the season. When we give our best effort, that is love in action. That love and service to our team could separate us from being good to possibly great.

March 7

Travel

Coach Cole has done a really good job with our team considering that this is his 1st season. Travel is a major responsibility of his.

Heading to Conway—This is the first time we would fly to UCA. Robin was waiting in Little Rock for us. Plan on 8:30 a.m. flight—ABI airport calls at 7 a.m. that we are about to miss our flight. Coach Cole looks back thru many emails from travel agent to find a change in flight time. He had not noticed it in a trail of emails. We missed our flight. Looked at lots of different options in about a 45-minute time slot and decided to get another bus to head towards Robin. Asked Robin to head to Texas and pick us up in East Texas.

The first bus breaks down 10 miles outside of Abilene. Wait an hour for bus #2. Watch "The Help" on DVD, then stop for lunch. Get back on bus after lunch and DVD will not pop out of DVD player. We watch "The Help" again!!

Met Robin somewhere east of DFW. Arrive in Conway at UCA at 8 p.m. After departing Abilene at 8 a.m. 12-hour trip is not setting team up for success in game the following day v UCA (who nearly beat us at home)!!

March 2

Won 67–65

We do not allow players to make excuses and blaming terrible travel the day before a game would be no exception.

Our team—Played so hard. Struggled to have legs under 3-pt. shots (4 made 3s). Also a step slow on defense—gave up lots of middle drives.

Brea played so hard and smart like her usual self, but struggled to score. 1 of 7 scoring. Her 4 assists were huge.

We had to score in our final possession, being tied 65–65 w/ time for UCA to get the ball back.

I call a play for Brea to drive in for a layup off, but backs ball out to set up a Madi Miller backdoor cut! Madi makes layup! We then needed one defensive stop to get this win—We got it! We sweep UCA, big success to sweep such a good program.

In the locker room, I tell team how proud I am that they **"Controlled the Controllables"**—*persevered, stayed focused, fought 'til final buzzer, moved on to the next play all night and didn't feel sorry for themselves about bad travel.*

Hopped on the bus and yes drove home (in less than 8 hours!).

Our team exuded championship level toughness this weekend.

March 9

Sara's Day
Senior Day

This player! Sara has evolved into a vocal leader, pretty hard worker and fierce competitor. I don't know how much she loves to win, but she hates the consequence of losing.

She has embraced TEAM and understands that the more she invests, the more she reaps. TEAM success has become her focus.

And her desire and focus to live out her "One Word"— FINALE—in a grand fashion are allowing her to truly leave a legacy.

Hoping the day is wonderful for her and that our team honors her with great effort today!

Postgame:

Sara's final home game is incredible—she has a double double with 12 pts and a career high 12 assists! 5 players scored in double digits and 16 made 3s later, we have a dominant win over UIW 102–53. Great "Sara Day" and great momentum to carry us into Katy for Conference tourney.

Will face SAM-UCA Winner, as 4 seed. Need revenge on SAM. Know we can defeat UCA. We will prepare to play either opponent—we have no preference.

Big Week of Preparation—Convince players to focus on 1 game at a time, but be tough enough to win 3 games in a row.

March 10

Spring Break didn't hurt our crowd too much for the final regular season game, final home game and Sara's last game in Moody!

Sam Houston loss was painful but proved to be one of the most beneficial hurdles of the season!

It's really hard to beat a team 3 times, but that will be the task in tourney if we face UCA. Kamry Orr has gotten the best of us in our 2 games this year, but our team prevailed both times to win the games.

*Preparations for the week should be efficient, high tempo, intense but light as well. Light hearted and burden free. We need to get better—**Godly Women Striving for Excellence**—bring our best version everyday but have plenty of fire and competitive spirit to take with us. We don't play until Friday so time for maintenance and plenty of video.*

Last season our focus was on playing in our 1st ever SLC Tournament. We accomplished that and won a game as well. We are now more mature and are set on winning 3 games this tournament.

We will focus on what we can control. With our FAMILY shirts from Nike we have a great reminder that this journey has been and will continue to be about Family—about our culture and relationships on the team. We will either make history this week or we won't, but either way we will do this as a FAMILY!

March 17

A.M.	Position Workout
P.M.	Team Workout, Weights, Cold Tub

Hit it hard early in the week then we will taper off. Have legs, hearts and minds ready for Friday.

March 12

Individual skill workouts, then 1-hr team workout. Video of our UIW game—highlighted the great team offense! Need to play together as a team this week—be willing to make extra pass, set better, bigger screens, crash offensive boards relentlessly to keep ball at our end. We have proven all year to be a great shooting team, but offensive rebounds afford us more opportunities to score.

March 13

Last team practice in Moody before tourney—surely not last practice!! Are the blessings we have experienced so far all that we will receive this season?! If so, we have had favor on us for sure and it has been a tremendous year! If not, if there is more in store for this team, let us live out our verse, Galatians 6:9, as we board the bus and take our fearlessness with us to Katy. We won't even realize what blessings are left on the table when we don't dream big. God is so Big and his plans are Gigantic!! No comfort zone now. We have to be bold enough to let God continue His mighty work through us.

March 13

In 2017 we had 3 all-conference selections in Alexis Mason, Suzzy Dimba and Lizzy Dimba.

And now we have that honor again, with Brea and Dom on the 2nd team and Sara on 3rd team.

I'm beyond proud of this group and believe that they are so well deserved of these awards.

Brea has been the hub of our team in that she plays with poise and makes everyone around her better. Dom has scored at all levels this season—in the paint, 3-point-land and the free throw line! My goodness she is so tough to guard. I know I sound like a broken record when I am asked about Sara, but she really is playing the best basketball of her career right now! She is so on point with reading defenses the past 5 or 6 games.

These 3 are going to be ready to lead our team to do something special in Katy. This is so exciting and it hasn't even started yet!

March 14

Arrived in time for dinner last night in Katy. Hotel was awesome at check in, great video room, team room, great rooms. Feeling good. When you look for everything to be great, things seem to turn out pretty well. Does it translate into wins—who knows but we are here with grateful hearts and ready to be the best we can be!

UCA v. Sam Houston game, at 11 a.m., so cool that we get to watch our next opponent. Players look amazing in new hoodies that have "OWNIT" on 1 sleeve and Gal. 6:9 on the other. Do not grow weary! I saw a random Tweet that was a great reminder to not get in God's way—"Don't put a period where God intended a comma."

The best is yet to come, Wildcats!!!!

Introduced **predator mindset**.

We cannot have a prey mentality where we hide from opponents. Our predator mindset will be eyes on the threat, face adversity head on, be the attackers, pursue greatness by being in control, relentless attack mode. No victims here!

Prey—rabbit, bird, squirrel—eyes on side
Predator—bear, wolf, tiger—eyes in front
*Eyes on the side—ready to hide (scared, looking for dangers)
*Eyes on the front—ready to hunt (attackers)
Predators—control what they can control, focus on what's

in front, not last play but next play, focus on attitude,
toughness, effort; fired up—ready to battle
Prey—Focus on what's going on around them—fans,
rankings, officials, worried, scared

We have earned our spot in the Tournament. Now we
should enjoy the experience with a predator mentality.

Attended the UCA/SHS Game as a Team

UCA had a huge 4th quarter to beat Sam Houston. Here
we go—Round 3 vs. UCA! Coach Rushing is an excellent
coach and will have her team ready to go!

They play in-your-face tough half-court defense. We have
to take care of the ball and be shot ready. If they force
drives, we have to make our layups. Take what they give
us, whether it's layups or 3s—Let's Go!

Teams that go to Katy with the most confidence, are on
the same page and are sharing the same goals will be the
most successful! We couldn't have scripted a more perfect
final regular season game than last Saturday. We will
ride the momentum of that game into this tournament
quarterfinal. We have nothing to lose and have as
good of a chance to win it all as anyone else! **TEAM
FIRST WINS!**

March 15

Friday 11:00 AM, Quarter finals vs. UCA

YES—overflowing with amazement, appreciation and pride for this team!

[Pretournament goal was to set a 3-point record in tournament. We knew what some 3-point records were, but didn't specify what we would do or what game it would happen. I have done UCA scout for several seasons and know their coach game plans to take away our 3s and force drives so I really didn't know what the 3-pt. game would look like in this matchup.]

Result: New 3-pt. Tourney records—Most atts—35, Most made 16!

7 different players made 3s, led by Brea with 4! Makayla, Kam, and Madi all hit 3! 20 assists for our team—great effort to share the basketball!

The casual fan may have wondered why we were running up the score. It wasn't about that at all! This wasn't even about the opponent. We were locked in on a team goal and doing something special in the SLC from the 3-point line! I couldn't say "Stop shooting"—that's just not us!

We had spent 4 days starving distractions so that we could be our best. We eliminated anything, any thought that might prevent us from being extremely focused.

Control the Controllables.

We made no secret of the fact that we wanted to break some tournament records, we did a lot of things really well throughout the game. We shared the ball so well and our shooters were all shot ready, which led to 20 assists! We also played very intense team defense.

FRI NIGHT
ACU Men's Semifinal vs. Southeastern La.

We get to the arena just after tipoff. When we walked in as a team (dressed alike!) our fans erupted cheering for us! I held back tears hard. We waved and couldn't believe the reception.

[ACU Houston set up a tailgate for fans before the games. SLC official said this is the first group to ever tailgate at the tourney. TRENDSETTERS. I hope lots of fans are going to those.]

The guys played like Warriors! So, so proud—they battled all night and beat Southwestern Louisiana. Championship Bound! Now more emotion for them *winning and about to go to bed the night before we play our own semifinal vs LAMAR!!!*

The guys have a little more pressure to win tomorrow being the higher seed. Not us! Not one person outside of our team room expects ACU to beat Lamar!

We will have the team ready! When the game starts, many would say there is only so much that a coach can do. I agree, to a certain extent, and that's why our role is so big in the preparation. We have to have minds right to make the best decisions tomorrow. Be ready to stay confident in all circumstances!! DO NOT GROW WEARY in doing what is right!

March 16

Pregame breakfast awesome!
Players alert, anxious for game time.
Everyone knows keys to the game vs. a talented team like Lamar—"Don't let what you can't do prevent you from doing what you can do!"—John Wooden

Take care of the ball—everyone has to embrace that.

Lamar scores quickly after steals—one of the nation's leaders in steals—led by Chastadie Barrs (best in the country).

Make them guard our half-court offense. (They will try to get us to play fast and take quick shots.)

Rebound on both ends (give them limited extra possessions).

Must get defensive stops. We CAN also score quickly in transition!

We Won. 88–79 v. Lamar

Came back from being down—down the entire 1st half and finally outscored them in the 3rd quarter to get within 6 pts going into the 4th!

*We play from behind in drills, workouts, and scrimmages vs. our male scout team. We know it isn't over 'til the final buzzer. Go hard no matter what—**GRIT DON'T QUIT! TEAM FIRST WINS! OWN IT!***

The sheer focus and determination was incredible! Players on the bench, players in huddles, breathing life and encouragement into each other. This team ran low on fuel in the 1st half but gathered themselves and showed great resolve and persistence as they became predators in the 2nd half.

Unbelievable belief and focus by these fearless ladies to turn the table on a talented and aggressive Lamar team who has 2 of the best players in the league leading them.

Once we finished 3rd quarter, you could just feel a swing of momentum and confidence from our squad.

4th quarter—all about us getting defensive stops. Brea or Sara deflections, a big rebound by Dom or Madi, or a Makayla 3 off an extra pass in transition.

One of the most complete and dominant quarters this team has ever played! This is a physical game for sure, but it's the hearts and souls of our players that won this semi-final, upset #1 seed, and is sending us to our 1st EVER SLC championship!!

This is one of the gutsiest performances and best wins of any team I have coached at ACU! We withstood the challenge of battling one of the nation's top defensive teams!

Our team missed only 2 free throws the entire game. 28 made free throws is now a new record in the DI era for our program, with 20 of 20 made in the fourth quarter alone!

I'm so proud of our team and excited to coach the 1st ACU Women's Basketball Team to play in an SLC Tournament Championship game!

The players really trusted what we asked them to do. They believed going into the 4th quarter that we had a chance to win.

This team just wanted to win this game, no matter what and that was their mentality 'til the final buzzer!

March 17

SLC Championship vs. Texas A&M Corpus Christi (1st Ever SLC Championship Appearance)

I wake up this morning feeling like I have already coached the game—spent hours during the night watching plays executed perfectly in my mind. It probably won't look as neat today as I visualized it, but I am full of confidence in our game plan, our players' abilities, my staff and in our fans—who will for sure energize us through any rough moments today.

In total transparency, I didn't ask a coach to have TAMCC scout report ready because they were the 6 seed. It is so difficult to win 3 days in a row, but the Islanders, led by Royce Chadwick, have done just that. They deserve to be in this final, just as much as we do, because of the fearless determination which they are exuding in this tourney.

My assistant, Drew Cole, had my back! He had the scout for TAMCC and he was prepared to present it to our team after we won the semifinal! My assistants are the best!

*Side note before we play this game:

I played 2 seasons of junior college ball at Western Texas College for Royce's dad, Kelly Chadwick. Coach Chadwick was the hardest coach I played for as far as discipline, attention to detail, being critical and basketball intelligence—off the chart. But I learned so much from him. He passed away in Sept of 2013. I know somehow he will be following this game today very closely.

Winners! Goodness Gracious!

What a crazy game! We were up 22 pts at halftime. TAMCC made runs in the first half, but our offensive execution was so good and shooters were shot ready every time they got open.

Then it was as if the rim all of a sudden got smaller for us in the 3rd quarter. Corpus started hitting shots. Our misses and their defensive rebounds resulted in high percentage shots for them.

Our players (and even fans) could feel the game slipping away. Great example of no lead is ever big enough when you are playing a good team. Corpus was getting defensive stops and scoring off rebs and &1 shots in the paint. At that point I had to turn into my team's biggest cheerleader. They needed to know how much confidence I had in them and I had to continue encouraging communication even through adversity on the court. We had to get stops and make shots.

Lexie Ducat rebounded a missed FT (biggest rebound of the season!) and got the ball to Brea, who was fouled with only a few seconds left. Brea made FTs to give us a 69–66 advantage. TAMCC ended the game with yet another offensive rebound putback, but they needed 3 pts and not just 2! Winners! NCAA Tourney! We set NCAA tourney as our goal on June 1 and we have been bound and determined to make it a reality! Goal attained!

Both men's and women's teams will now play in March Madness. We rose to the occasion 3 straight days, 3 straight games, against 3 very different teams. I am so proud of this team and know they will continue to represent Wildcat Nation in a first-class manner!

*What a display of **TEAM FIRST WINS** in these 3 games! Our starters brought their best efforts for our team to be successful, not for their own glory. Then our reserves like Madi and Alyssa were on the edge of their chairs always ready to go in and contribute when called on. The players on the bench, whoever was there, were cheering, coaching,* and encouraging their teammates who were on the court in the battle. This team has embraced the philosophy of sacrificing self for something really special—for team success!

March 18

Well, "To be the best, you have to beat the best" just escalated to a crazy level.

We will play Baylor in the 1st Round of the NCAA Tournament. They are the #1 ranked 1 seed of the entire event. The #1 team in America!

They absolutely dominated the Big 12, while beating those opponents an average of 25 pts per game. This is why I have kept them at the top of my list when I place my vote each week as a poller for the USA Today Women's Basketball Coaches Poll. They are a phenomenal team with athletic scoring guards and the best post tandem in America with Cox and Brown. Let's Go!

This is actually best-case scenario for our fans—our 1st NCAA tourney experience will be played only 3 hrs. away, in Waco. Our fans will travel from all over Texas to cheer us on in this historic game.

Coach Kim Mulkey is one of the best WBB coaches of all time. They have won 9 straight Big 12 Championships!

Kim's leadership keeps her program in the top 5 in the country year in and year out.

*I feel like I'm not even thinking straight. This is so exciting while mind blowing all at the same time. Time to uber focus on **Control the Controllables**. Can't get distracted by the challenges in which we cannot control.*

March 20

As a staff, we are dividing and conquering the scouting report. There are so many components of how to game plan and what to emphasize. When preparing to go to battle against the best team in the country, we really need to focus on what our strengths are. Baylor is so dominant in every component of the game that we have to find a couple of things that we will focus on and emphasize that are in our control—regardless of the incredible size, speed and talent of Baylor.

As a staff working together on the report, we decided on our keys:

On Defense—

1. *Reduce number of transition points allowed—send 2 back on every shot, and take care of the basketball.*

2. *5 players must relentlessly pursue defensive rebounds.*

3. *Never let their posts score 1 on 1—must double team them on the catch-aggressive helpside.*

On Offense—

1. *Score in transition before Baylor sets up on defense. If we don't, then milk the shot clock.*

2. *Read the defense and value the ball.*

3. *Each player "echoes" called plays and sprints to get set up.*

4. *Must set strong screens!*

5. *Get the ball in the paint to kick to shooters.*

Baylor has some of the best players in the country so they are able to keep their offense fairly simple—post-feed and score in transition. Two aspects that I love and value as a coach, but don't know how we can deter them from doing either.

I know our players are excited about this huge challenge. We have to prepare them so well that when they step into this incredible battle, they will go with confidence, but also a sense of pride that they are the pioneers from ACU Women's Basketball embarking on an unfamiliar journey into the NCAA battlefield.

*We will have success and be able to walk away from this great feat, holding our heads up high as long as we give our best effort throughout the preps and the game. Give our very best to put **TEAM FIRST** and to bring glory to God and make Wildcat Nation proud!*

March 22

This was our shortest road trip of the year—the NCAA tournament—in WACO!

We enjoyed a good meal at the hotel tonight while we watched our men play Kentucky in the men's first round of the NCAA Tournament.

We cheered with each made shot, big rebound and steal. It was so cool listening to the commentators talk about the Wildcats and about ACU. How will the ACU exposure be measured for March Madness? Only 3 schools in America had both men's and women's basketball teams win their conference tournaments. That fact was mentioned a few times in the men's game.

After watching the courageous game played by our men, I shared a few thoughts with our team about what we can learn from seeing our men play.

We will have around 2000 ACU fans in the arena and we have to get them into the game—give them something to cheer about:

- *3s*
- *Hustle plays—charges, dive on loose balls*
- *Great teamwork*
- *Play to win—lots of energy from start to finish regardless of score*

We have been a good road team. We will have more ACU fans at this game than at any other road game this season! Everyone at our game is already proud of what we have accomplished so we have no pressure to impress but rather an opportunity to put ACU Women's Basketball on the NCAA Division I map!

Dom, Sara, Brea and I will speak at a press conference today before practice. We want our messages to be heard—

We are:

- *Godly women striving for excellence*
- *Grit don't quit*
- *Control the controllables*
- *Be excellent for Christ*
- *OWN IT—take responsibility for own actions, and put the we before the me*

March 23

We were defeated in every category on the stat sheet, but I am so proud of how our players handled themselves!

Along with ACU and Baylor were also University of California—Berkeley and the University of North Carolina at the site. The ACU fans came out today for us. Our purple section number was around 2500 in attendance. The 2 out-of-state schools had 100 or less per school. Now that's support for the Wildcats!

Our team was taken back by the presence of so many fans—it was unbelievable. We didn't give them much to cheer about but they were on the edges of their chairs, waiting for any little chance to stand up and clap for us!

We were not picked to finish even in the top 4 of our league and we just made history for ACU by playing in the NCAA tourney. This team exceeded all expectations of those outside of our own locker room!

I have a feeling that we just played the National Champions. I urged our team after the game in the locker room to cheer hard for Baylor throughout the rest of the tournament. We want them to bring the trophy back to Texas and we can say they had to go through ACU to get it!

Our 1st experience in the NCAA Tourney has been a wonderful one! Even though the opponent dominated us, I couldn't stop smiling! This was a 1st of great proportion. We are the only ACU WBB team that will be the 1st team to represent ACU on the big stage in March Madness. That is a forever fact!

Coach Mulkey was so hospitable, along with everyone at Baylor. We were treated very professionally and first class. Even our male scout team experienced March Madness by playing against Baylor's practice squad the day before our game. These guys were tremendous this season—showing up everyday to challenge us physically in practice. But even our scout team couldn't emulate the size and power of the awesome Baylor Bears. Wow—I sincerely hope they can win this title again! They have all the weapons to do so and the best coach in the country.

I don't know what will happen in the future for this ACU program, and I don't want to even concern myself with it now! I want to enjoy this experience as long as we possibly can. Who knows how long people will be talking about this season, but I'm sure we will enjoy every last conversation about it!

When I got back to our hotel room after the game, I was met with open arms by Rob and Macy. Bailey had a track meet in Abilene so she watched the game at home. We talked about how incredible the atmosphere in the arena was and how fun the whole trip had been. My brother and sister-in-law, Randy and Terri, were there, along with my parents, Conrad and Betty.

And then I shared my personal pregame issues with them. Everyone knew about Coach Golding's hole in his pants. It was talked about for days after his press conference.

I went to the bathroom pregame in our locker room while our team was warming up. I had a slight panic attack when I noticed that the thread had come out of the seam in the crotch of my black dress pants! I wouldn't be able to bend over or squat down coaching without the back of my pants gaping open. I hustled to Maya's training bag and grabbed athletic tape. I ran a long piece of tape along the seam to hold it together. At halftime the tape was still holding half of the seam together, so I applied another strip of tape that got me all the way through the game without an embarrassing incident. We laughed 'til we cried and realized that our family had just had a pretty dang special day.

WBB SEASON ENDS AT BAYLOR, BUT THE WILDCATS WILL RETURN

Women's Basketball

Posted: 3/23/2019 8:29:00 PM

"I'm so proud of our team," said Abilene Christian head coach Julie Goodenough during her postgame press conference. "People don't remember back in the fall, we were picked sixth in the Southland Conference, and here we are playing in the first-ever NCAA Tournament. Our team has really overcome a lot of odds and really exceeded expectations of everybody outside of our locker room.

"I can't say enough about our team and our program," she continued. This is our sixth year to play Division I and we have won three conference championships, so we feel like we're headed in the right direction.

"Dominique Golightly has been our leading scorer this year and she just has been tough as nails," said Goodenough. "She came so far from her sophomore year to her junior year.

"Breanna Wright has been starting point guard since her freshman year," added Goodenough, "and that kid just exudes toughness and confidence. Those two, with Sara, were the best guard trio in the Southland Conference this year, and I just really appreciate their leadership and them leading us to the NCAA Tournament."

A native of Rowlett, Texas, Williamson totaled four points vs. the Bears on 2–4 shooting to finish her senior campaign with a .617 field-goal percentage. She also goes into the ACU history books as the winningest Wildcat (88 wins) of their NCAA DI era and its first to win three conference rings in four seasons.

"I don't know if I have the words to describe it except I just feel honored and blessed," said Williamson about playing her final game in Purple and White. It has been a dream come true to play for ACU and under Coach Goodenough and alongside Brea and a couple of the other girls, it's been a heck of a ride. Three championships in my four years here, I would say is pretty successful, but I'll let you guys be the judge of that."

Kirgan was the Wildcats' leading scorer tonight with 10 points on 4–5 shooting in 18 minutes off the bench, while Golightly was the team's top rebounder with seven and Wright recorded three assists.

With the victory, Baylor advances to play Cal in the second round of the NCAA Championship Monday night.

The Berkeley Bears today eliminated North Carolina in Waco, 92–72, outscoring the Lady Tar Heels 81–50 over the first three quarters.

"We want to congratulate Baylor on such a great season and we wish them well," said Goodenough, who embraced her longtime coaching colleague during pre-game greetings. "We honestly are huge fans of Baylor and hope they go on and win the national championship.

"I love Kim Mulkey, and she does a great job with this program, and hopefully they will stay healthy and make a great run through the tournament and bring the national championship back to Texas."

Mulkey later returned the respect and adoration she has for Goodenough during her time with the media.

"I just have always liked Julie. She just—there's just some people you connect with, and I haven't seen her in a while. I connected with her when she was at Oklahoma State, and you know, there's just certain coaches you pull for, you really do. And I've just always pulled for her. We played them several years ago and she just does a good job.

"She (Julie) is everything that's good about women's basketball," said the two-time national championship winning coach (2005, 2012). "I loved her when she was at Oklahoma State. She's a family person. Those kids play hard for her. Those kids had a good year, and she's found in my opinion the place that she should stay until she retires."

Now that ACU is here in Waco and feeling the buzz of electricity that comes with being encircled by ESPN and grouped alongside DI royalty, Baylor, North Carolina and Cal, the Wildcats are not going to lose this taste for the champion environment.

It's permanently fused into their DNA.

They'll come back next season hungry to win, determined to cut down the nets in Katy, and push their way further through the field of 64. Just like ACU, it's worth knowing UConn also lost its first NCAA game in 1989, as did Baylor in 2001, and that it took the Gonzaga women 20 years to reach its first dance in 2007.

Since 1982 NCAA women's championship environments have been born and bred in small cities across the country: Storrs, Conn. (pop. 15,344), West Lafayette, Ind. (46,269) and Waco (136,436) and College Station (113,564) to name a few, so perhaps Abilene (121,885) will be next?

Maybe. But here's what her team has to first accomplish according to coach Goodenough.

"(If) we don't want to be considered a 16-seed anymore . . . we can't drop games at home in conference play," she said. "We need to beat somebody big, someone in a perceived higher conference than us. We need to win the conference championship, the regular season, and we need to win the tournament so that we're not a 16-seed next year.

"We want to be able to jockey our position a little bit at the NCAA Tournament where we can win a ballgame, and as long as we're 16, it's going to be really, really hard. I think being a 15 will be pretty tough.

"The conversation we'll have with our players in the off-season and the summer is, 'We can't be okay with dropping games at home in conference play and we have to win games that we're not supposed to win. We've got to beat somebody we're not supposed to beat.'"

Copyright 2019 Abilene Christian University Athletics

Written by Chris Macaluso, assistant director of athletics for media relations, immediately following the game, portions used with permission.

3 weeks following the end of our season we hosted our annual Women's Basketball Celebration Banquet. These are the notes from my presentation:

ACU BASKETBALL BANQUET

Our CELEBRATION of another amazing Season!!

April 14, 2019

Gal 6:9 from the Message says:

> So let's not allow ourselves to get fatigued doing good. At the right time we will harvest a good crop if we don't give up, or quit. Right now, every time we get the chance, let us work for the benefit of all.

Great reflection of how this team battled this season! **Here to Celebrate!**

***Thank You to ACU** for allowing me to be your head wbb coach and for allowing me the freedom to honor God through Coaching. Wow a priv! and a special THANK YOU to my new boss—**Allen Ward** for ensuring that I will be here a few more years.

Wonderful crowd! Thanks to you =our **fans, friends, and families**-you have walked alongside us this whole season! And we thank you for your love & support. Your attendance tonight =another sign of your continued support for our team.

- Thank you to the **ACU fac/staff and ACU athletics dept folks** who are here! Appr your yearlong investment in our program.
  - Acad support **Krista Masci/ Jonathon Stewart—thank you**
  - *Sports info crew*—**Chris-print, Seth-video, Zach-voice—really good representing our team-THANKS!**
- Thank you to the **WILDCAT CLUB** members for your support thru gifts
- **Another super special group to our program are our wonderful MENTORS**
- Our players and our staff really appreciate what **you all** do for us throughout the year—you cheer for us, Pray, provide meals and snacks, celebrate with us, –these actions are part of the **ACU DIFF**! The way you treat our players like family is *EXTRAordinary!* Doesn't happen everywhere. **THANK YOU!**

- ***Special Thank you =- Paul Kim, & Sydney,** loved& appreciated   **ROB-Can't put into words my gratefulness for your support. Thank you for sharing ideas and inspirations-(JH)** Sharing the adventure w/you makes it even more fun!
- **Bailey, Macy, Ava, and Mya** You have to sacrifice a lot for this team-we love you so much for that. Ask that you be good big sisters to our newest member, **Tatum!**

Thank you to my incredible staff: A head coach is only as good as their staff!!

Blessed w/ staff of great character and integrity

manager—Chris Garcia **all girl supervisor** Macy— Thanks so much!

ROBIN WALLS—Best Bus driver ever—SLC champion bus driver—great friend of ours as well

Maya Natori—ath trainer

My coaching staff: COMPLIMENT EACH OTHER WELL

Drew Cole—Director of travel, academic liaison, facilities coord, and post dev coach

Erik DeRoo—Creative Recruiting Coordinator, Video coordinator, Scout team supervisor, Pt Gd Dev Coach, dad to TATUM

Erika Lambert—Assoc head coach, Recr Coord, Post dev coach,

Alumni outreach & Comm Service coord-organizing events—like this banquet

BEST STAFF in the SLC!! THANK you all so much!

Blessed with another incredible season. WISE friend encouraged me to take notes on the season-we were both anticipating a special one—Thanks Dr McCaleb ☺

Began in June 2018 =Growing our team including camps, Workouts, team activities

Building the culture-1 of <u>excellence</u>=Be the best version of yourself—a daily task.

<u>John Wooden says</u>-Do not let what you cannot do, interfere with what you can do.

OUR CULTURE: Controlling the Controllables! Team 1st WINS!

Focus on controllables -great energy, positive attitude, selfless communication, must work on culture daily!!! #OWNIT-be responsible!

- —**preseason SLC poll we were picked 6th** haha-great bulletin board material!!!!
- —Tough non-conference season—6 -0 wins at NMSU and UTEP/hosted ARK-1st SEC at home
- —Christmas break=terrible game at Tech ☹ responded though by starting SLC play at 5–1

5 road games—1 home game vs McNEESE. score– 109–52= est. 3 DI records-109 pts scored, 45 FGM, 27 assts.

__FEB__-rough start lost 2 at home-Lamar by 3/ lost to a scrappy Sam Houston team

following SHSU loss-had a lengthy mtg in the locker room-**1.5 hr tm mtg-**

DEFINING MOMENT —How we responded to this adversity would define the rest of the season

Next game was at HSU (Sing Song week)

- —**at HSU v NU**—broken door knob!!! Best thing ☺
- —God thing!!! 5 str wins after this!!

Small victories-SWEPT UIW (102, & 109-top 2 highest scoring games **in SLC)**

Beat UCA 3xs including at Conway—12 hours and 3 buses to get there!!

Beat CORPUS 3xs!! HUGE!!

—Competed in **only 2nd SLC conf tourney** (bye the 1st rd!!)

Set a new standard-don't play 1st day!

In case you weren't able to be in KATY or you need a reminder:

+VS UCA—scored 82 vs while setting new 3 pt record —16 of 35

+VS CONF champ-Lamar—trailed going into 4th—score 36 pts in the 4th= **BREA-16–16 FTS**

+VS A&M CC—big lead-then we withstood a valiant comeback -but never trailed/ came down to <u>**one**</u> of the biggest off rebs **Dom** got her own/ THEN **<u>THE biggest</u>** off reb of the season for sure—**Lexie Ducat!** Brea makes both FTS!!!

Led to **<u>1st EVER SLC Tourney championship!</u>**

1st NCAA Tourn! Fun selection show in the stadium club level.

Game will be in Waco—Best possible location for our fans!

Baylor!!! Not scared!! So prepared!! Played the eventual 2019 Natl Champs

—**STAT sheet**=

Led conf-**3s att, 3s made(40th) 3s mpg (pg 43rd) R Mar (38th)**

FG% (18th) Assists 17 apg(23rd) pts Sc-73 (50th)

Introduce our players—please stand and remain standing w/your class

FRESH:—<u>ONE WORD</u>

<u>**Kamryn-circumspective**</u>—suffered inj-has a bright future as floor leader **9 pts (3) v UCA**

<u>**Diamond**</u>—process quite a gem—hard worker—made huge strides this season **44%FG**

<u>**Madi**</u>—**relentless** 6th-7th man this season, **sc. 9pts 4xs(UCA)** plays so hard!

GAME winner at UCA on backdoor cut!!

Soph: stand

<u>**Josie Larson**</u>—**serve** kind heart—great 3 pt shooting threat for us **48%!!**

<u>**Makayla Mabry**</u>—**consistent**—2nd FT%, one of top 3 pt shooters, #10 reb **17pts v UTEP**

<u>**Alyssa Adams**</u>—**patience** driver, FT shooter and reb, **14 pts** @UIW

Anna McLeod—Conquer—blessed to have Anna —ready-fun & scorer!

JRS: stand

Pam Herrera—peace—chaotic schedule—nursing school, 42% **fg** hard worker on & off crt

Lexi Kirgan-fearless—big inside presence, finished season strong—**6 fgm v UIW/**

leading scorer 12 **pt v Baylor**

C—Lexie Ducat-craft—Hon Mention POW 2xs, 11 ppg (**1 of 4 DD scores**) +6 rpg, (**11th SLC**) **not surprising=for AÇU** *1st off reb -2.8=Inc off reb vs TAMCC!!, hard nosed*

C-Dominique Golightly purposeful—Hon M POW 5xs, excel shooter top 5 in SLC in all 3pt stats 2nd in scoring **13.4(13th SLC)** 3rd leading reb-**5.8(16 SLC)**

C—Brea Wright-relax—HM POW2xs, scores layups, 3s, & FTS!

13.8 leading scorer (**10 SLC**) 2nd in ast/**4.7 3rd in SLC (66in USA)**

SRS: Sara Williamson-finale—Where to start ☺ HM POW 4xs 3rd
11.9 pts(19 SLC) led ACU in **assts 4.8 (2nd slc) 61** in nation!

Locker room sign—Those who stay who will be
champions! Sara—3x Conf Champion
CAREER—DI era—most games played **125**

Most games won—**88**   Grad in May!!
Thanks so much! SARA! *Whatever you do, whatever
your job, =, Do your job in such a way that God is
glorified. ***Life is too short to settle for average!**

FANS of the YEAR—2nd season for this award—thank
you ALL for making this a tough choice!!!
Our award winning couple has stepped up for our
team in many ways from prayers, to cheering at our
games, financial support, texts of encouragement and
congratulations, and constantly asking what else can we
do for you and the team.

Women's basketball FANS of the Year =Rick and Debbie Wessel

(Jen is here in Debbie's place)

Team Season awards:

Rebs	6.2 10th SLC <u>Makayla</u>
3 pt made per game	2.1 5th SLC 149th <u>Dominique</u>
FT%	88% 2nd SLC #18 in country—<u>Brea</u>
FG%	61.7 1st in SLC #8 in the country
	just ahead of Baylor's Kalani Brown—<u>Sara</u>

No job is not your job Award—Affectionately named "Byrd Award"—

after Cailyn Byrd—served our team for 5 seasons in whatever capacity we needed her
Inaugural winner for the **BYRD award**—selfless—what else, what can I do—**Kamryn Mraz**

CONF awards

2nd team All-academic—Dominique
2nd team All-academic —Breanna
3rd Team All-conference—Sara
2nd Team all conf—Breanna
2nd Team all conf—Dominique
SLC All Tourney—Sara
SLC Tourney MVP—Breanna

The future is really bright for us!
I am confident in this amazing group of returners—
Are returning=81 % of our scoring/ 90% rebounding

LOOK forward to 19–20,

Where we will <u>NOT DEFEND</u> our title as Champions but rather ATTACK the contenders!!

APPENDIX

ACU Women's Basketball Final Stats

23-10 (13-5)

Southland Tournament Champions
1st Ever NCAA Tournament Bid

STAT:	CONFERENCE:	COUNTRY:
3's / Game	1st (8.0)	39th
Total 3's Made	1st (265)	35th
Rebound Margin	1st (+5.9)	24th
Field Goal %	1st (45.8%)	15th
Assists / Game	2nd (16.7)	23rd

Individual Conference Stats:
3 All-Conference Guards
4 Players in Top 25 in Scoring
3 Players in Top 25 in Rebounding
2 Players in Top 25 in Assists and A/TO
SLC Tournament Record – FT % (16-16)

Team Conference Stats:
Top 2 Highest Scoring in Southland Games (109 & 102)
Top 2 High FG Made in Southland Games (45 & 40)
Top in 3's Made in a Southland Game (16)
SLC Tournament Record – 3's Made/ATT. (16-35)
3rd in Total Offense: 73.2 PPG
5th in Total Defense: 64.1 PPG Allowed

2018–19 Mentors

Mentor	**Player(s)**
Denise Barnett	Alyssa, Anna
Sheila Barton	Makayla
Micky Brewer	Sara
Sarah Ferguson	Pam
Aliza Gomez	Lexie
Shelby Hanigan	Kam
Kendra Hassell	Jenna
Mary-Margaret Johnson	Lexi, Madi
Michelle Overman	Brea
Mary Powell	Dom
Amanda Ramos	Kayla
Debi Shultz	Jazz
Judy Siburt	Diamond
Cristi Stanton	Josie

2018–19 Practice Team

Michael Allman
Shaun Biddix
Matt Ferriera
Andrew Graves
Andy McGrew
David Oputo
Malcolm Robertson
Tony Serna
Shea Southers
Conor Widder

NAME	WORD	SCRIPTURE
Alyssa Adams	Patience	"Always be humble and gentle. Be patient with each other, making allowance for each other's faults because of your love." —Eph. 4:2
Lexie Ducat	Craft	"Whatever you do, work at it with all your heart, as working for the Lord and not for men." —Col. 3:23
Dominique Golightly	Purposeful	"Commit your work to the Lord, and your plans will be established." —Prov. 16:3
Pam Herrera	Peace	"But the fruit of the spirit is love, joy, peace, forbearance, kindness, goodness, faithfulness.." —Gal. 5:22
Lexi Kirgan	Fearless	"For I, the Lord your God, will hold your right hand, saying to you, "Fear not, I will help you." —Isaiah 41:13
Josie Larson	Serve	"For even the Son of Man did not come to be served, but to serve, and give his life as a ransom for many." —Mk 10:45
Makayla Mabry	Consistent	"My covenant will I not break, nor alter the thing that is gone out of my lips." —Ps. 89:34
Anna McLeod	Conquer	"The Lord is my light and my salvation- whom shall I fear? The Lord is the stronghold of my life-of whom should I be afraid?" —Ps. 27:1
Madi Miller	Relentless	"No discipline seems pleasant at the time, but painful. Later on, however, it produces a harvest of righteousness and peace for those who have been trained by it." —Heb. 12:11

NAME	WORD	SCRIPTURE
Kamryn Mraz	Circum-spective	"Do not be conformed to this world, but be transformed by the renewal of your mind, that by testing you may discern what is the will of God, what is good and acceptable and perfect." —Rom. 12:2
Diamond Willcot	Process	"Let us not grow weary in doing good, for at the proper time we will reap a harvest if we do not give up." —Gal. 6:9
Sara Williamson	Finale	"But I do not account my life of any value nor as precious to myself, if only I may finish my course and the ministry that I received from the Lord Jesus, to testify to the gospel of the grace of God." —Acts 20:24
Breanna Wright	Relax	"Cast all your anxiety on him because he cares for you." —I Pet. 5:7

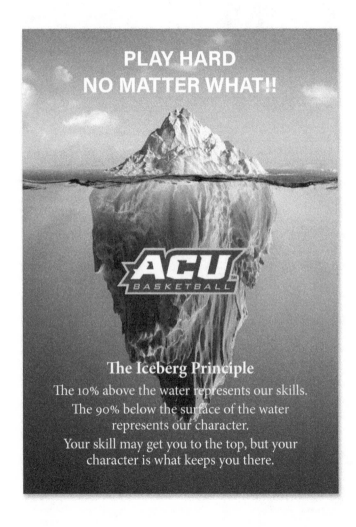

WOMEN'S BASKETBALL
CORE VALUES PYRAMID

MISSION

GODLY WOMEN STRIVING FOR EXCELLENCE

MOTTO

TEAM FIRST WINS

ACCOUNTABLE
- BE WHERE YOUR FEET ARE
- MAXIMIZE THE PRESENT
- GREAT TEAMS PURSUE GREATNESS TOGETHER

RESPECTFUL
- MOOD DOES NOT DICTATE MANNERS
- LEAVE A PLACE BETTER THAN YOU FOUND IT
- WALK ON SIDEWALKS WHEN AVAILABLE
- LOOK PEOPLE IN THE EYE AND SPEAK POLITELY

LOYALTY TO THE TEAM & ACU
- BE ALL IN
- REPLACE HAVE TO WITH GET TO
- ALWAYS AND IN ALL WAYS SPEAK POSITIVELY ABOUT ACU

INTEGRITY
- NO EXCUSES
- BE THE BEST VERSION OF YOURSELF
- BE THANKFUL, NOT WHINY

CONTROL THE CONTROLLABLES
- BE PART OF THE SOLUTION, NOT THE PROBLEM
- OWN YOUR ATTITUDE, ENERGY, AND COMMUNICATION

SELFLESS
- NO JOB IS NOT YOUR JOB
- PUT WE BEFORE ME

GRIT
- WORK OUTSIDE OF YOUR COMFORT ZONE
- EMBRACE THE TOO
- DEMONSTRATE CONSISTENT TOUGHNESS

JULIE GOODENOUGH

Head Women's Basketball Coach

A veteran head coach with 26 years of experience—and conference champion at the NAIA, DI, DII and DIII levels—Julie Goodenough recently completed a successful seventh season in leading the Abilene Christian women's basketball program to its fourth straight postseason.

Her 2015-16 and 2016-17 teams each qualified for the WNIT, with the program's first WNIT win, which was over Oklahoma State in 2017. Last year's squad made its Southland Conference Championship debut and posted an 88–66 first-round win over New Orleans.

Goodenough's Wildcat tenure began with a 2012–13 Lone Star Conference regular-season championship and accompanying Coach of the Year Award. Since bringing her team into the Southland Conference, they've rattled off six consecutive DI winning seasons.

Goodenough's ACU record is 144-68 (.676). (Prior to the conclusion of the 19-20 season.)

She won her 300th game as a collegiate head coach on Jan. 15, 2013 against UIW, and claimed win No. 400 in Las Vegas on Dec. 22, 2017 vs. the Lady Monarchs.

Goodenough was a 2007 inductee into the HSU Sports Hall of Fame in recognition of her nine-year 188–54 record, leaving as the winningest coach in school history. Her last four teams advanced to at least the NCAA Division III Sweet 16 and she also coached her team to the NAIA national tournament in her first two seasons.

Goodenough was the head coach at Hardin-Simmons University from 1993–2002 before going to Oklahoma State for three seasons. She was then the head coach at NCAA Division I Charleston Southern from 2006–12, where twice she led her team to the WBI.

She was a 2019 inductee into the Big Country Athletic Hall of Fame.

A 1991 graduate of Texas-Arlington, Goodenough and her husband, Rob, have two daughters, Bailey (ACU '18, '19) and Macy (ACU '20).